Child Labour
in
Morocco's Carpet Industry

An Anti-Slavery Society Report
1978

Published May 1978 by the Anti-Slavery Society
180 Brixton Road,
London SW9 6AT, England

Printed by The Russell Press
45 Gamble Street
Nottingham NG7 4ET, England

ISBN: 0 900918 06 3

Contents

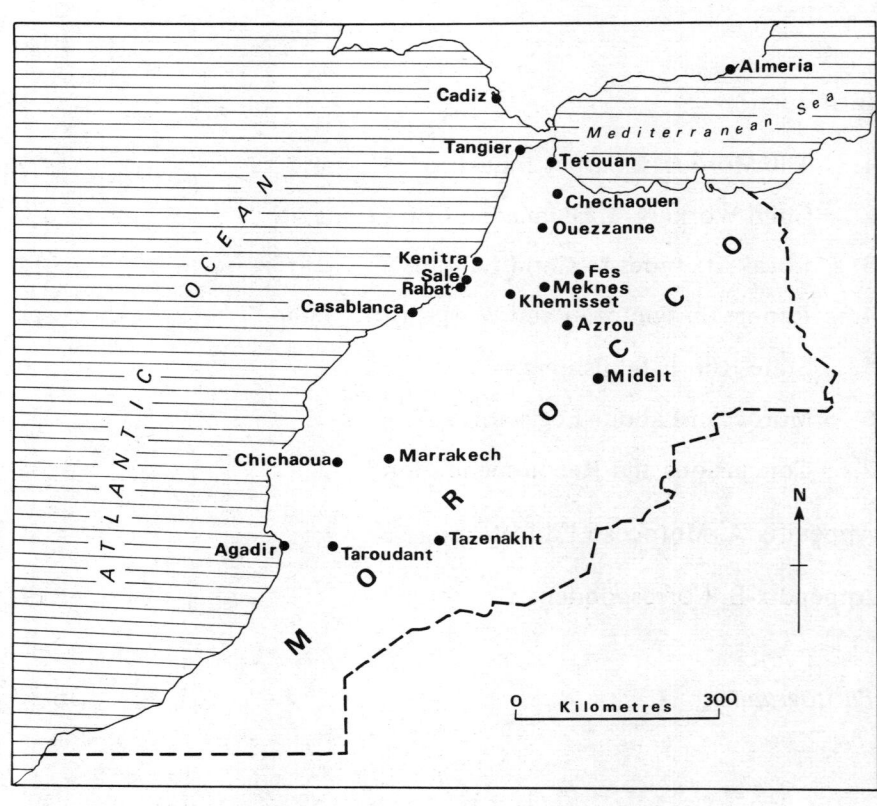

Almeria

Cadiz

Mediterranean *Sea*

Tangier

Tetouan

Chechaouen

ATLANTIC *OCEAN*

Ouezzanne

Kenitra

Salé
Rabat

Casablanca

Fes

Meknes
Khemisset

Azrou

Midelt

Chichaoua

Marrakech

Agadir

Taroudant

Tazenakht

M   O   R   O   C   C   O

N

0   Kilometres   300

Introduction

In March 1975, following reports of large-scale employment of children in carpet factories in Morocco, the Anti-Slavery Society sent a small team to investigate the situation. The team visited six factories of various sizes, one private embroidery workshop, two state cooperatives and one state school of apprenticeship.

They found that children aged from 5 upwards were permanently employed there, some for up to 12 hours a day and often in very bad conditions. They noted that the children were not employed directly by the factory owners, but worked for an intermediary — a *maalema* (craftswomen/supervisor) — who was herself paid on a piecework basis by the factory owners.

The team also noted the increasing demand for Moroccan carpets, the large numbers of girls not attending school and the consequent ready supply of cheap labour.

Feeling that this situation was detrimental both to the small girls involved and to the well-being of the whole country, the Anti-Slavery Society sent the team's report to the Moroccan government on 8 May 1975 and urged it to take steps to improve the working conditions of these girls. It believed that such improvements would only marginally affect the marketability of Moroccan rugs. Another letter was sent to the Moroccan government on 3 October 1975 stating that the report had been given to the UN Sub-Commission on Prevention of Discrimination and Protection of Minorities and also handed to the International Labour Organization. The Anti-Slavery Society offered to publish the government's comments along with the report.

The Moroccan government replied to the Anti-Slavery Society at the beginning of 1976. Pointing out the existence of legislation protecting all workers, including those in carpet factories, it stressed that the employment or apprenticeship of children under 12 was illegal.

In view of the Anti-Slavery Society's report, the Moroccan government accepted that in "a few" establishments these laws were not strictly applied, and it stated its intention to investigate the firms mentioned and ensure that in future the laws were obeyed.

The government felt that the fact that "a few" employers did not obey the laws should not lead to the hasty conclusion that such practices were widespread.

The unfavourable publicity that would result from publishing what they considered was not an objective study would, they felt, be prejudicial to Morocco's "considerable efforts" in this field.

The Anti-Slavery Society therefore waited a further year and in March 1977 sent out another small team to see to what extent the situation had improved. This Arabic-speaking team visited 62 private premises and 17 state centres in 17 cities and towns throughout Morocco.

The team found that the situation, far from having improved, had worsened. The custom of employing young girls under the legal age of 12 is now widespread. Hours of work often far exceed the legal maximum and paid annual holidays, medical visits and the official minimum salaries are hardly ever provided.

The second team's report was also sent to the Moroccan government through its embassy in London. This was on 17 June 1977. An accompanying letter again invited the government's comments and offered to publish them with the report.

When no reply to the letter was received by the end of the year, the Anti-Slavery Society decided to publish the 1977 report with an additional appendix containing facsimiles of the most pertinent correspondence with the embassy (see pages 60-71), omitting acknowledgement and reminders.

Although only the more comprehensive 1977 report is published here, we are publishing the Moroccan government's comments on the 1975 report in the absence of its comments on the 1977 report and because we believe they are important.

For publication, the Anti-Slavery Society has made some minor editorial and stylistic changes in the text sent to the Moroccan government and has incorporated most of the previous appendices into the main body of the report. It also has deleted a few footnotes which referred to instances when the second team was unable to confirm relatively minor details contained in the first report.

The conclusions and recommendations by the second team and by the Anti-Slavery Society, originally contained in the introduction, are now found at the end of the report.

Notes

Where the ages of children are not specifically stated, "very young" is used in the text to mean they are about 7 or 8. "Young" means aged between 8 and 12.

DH = dirham, the Moroccan currency.
The approximate exchange rate in April 1977 was 4.5DH to one US dollar.

A dahir is a Moroccan legal decree.

K = *Register of Moroccan Industry and Commerce, "Kompass",* 3rd edition, 1975/76.

Maalema (craftswoman/supervisor) is used here for both the singular and plural.

1. The Moroccan Carpet Industry

The Moroccan carpet trade has always played an important part in the economy of the country, where several regional styles have developed. Recently, however, it has been winning an increasing share of the export market. In 1972, carpets accounted for 53.8% of craft exports. In 1973, this figure had risen to 72.2%, to drop back again to 59% in 1974. In terms of value in Moroccan dirhams (DH), however, the rise has been steady:

1972 (in thousands of DH)	58,700
1973 (in thousands of DH)	81,746
1974 (in thousands of DH)	88,894
1975 (in thousands of DH)	113,067

Source: Direction de l'Artisanat – latest figures available in April 1977

With this increase in production there has been a consequent increase in the industrialization of an activity that was originally carried out in small workshops. Many companies now work solely for export, with large factories in several different towns.

Government policy is to give all possible aid to exporters of rugs: wool is imported duty free ("temporary importation") on condition that it is exported in the form of rugs. Export duty and certain taxes are waived.

West Germany is the greatest importer of Moroccan rugs and acts as re-distributor throughout Europe. Many firms the team visited were booked far into the the future with West German orders. By all accounts the trade is booming, especially as labour legislation and resulting higher prices put other competing countries out of the market. Algeria used to be the most important rug producer in North Africa but it was said that, with nationalization of the carpet firms, their prices had risen.

Most Moroccan manufacturers consider that Morocco is now in first place for North African rugs and many did not hide the fact that low labour costs made Moroccan rugs highly competitve. In Iran, for instance, legislation forbids the employment of children under 14 and this has considerably raised the cost of Persian rugs.

7

The distribution of the carpet trade by region is given in the following table, based on the official lead seal applied to each Moroccan rug before it can be exported. This government seal is intended as a guarantee of quality. Traditional and modern rugs are counted together and the surface figures are in thousands of square metres. The figures for 1976 do not include December.

	1974 Surface	1975 Surface	1976 Surface
Rabat	505.4	643.0	700.2
Salé	0.8	0.8	0.5
Kenitra	51.6	48.9	69.0
Casablanca	34.0	47.2	47.2
Fez	65.5	70.3	104.7
Meknès	22.7	31.6	40.3
Azrou	5.5	5.2	4.5
Marrakesh	62.2	46.7	64.6
Chichaoua	1.0	0.1	0.6
Ouarzazate	1.0	1.7	1.1
Taznakht	0.3	0.2	0.3
Tangier	246.7	296.3	345.4
Tetuan	1.2	4.1	0.9
Khemisset	4.6	2.2	0.3
Agadir	2.5	3.6	3.7
Oujda	1.4	0.9	0.3
Total	1,006.4	1,202.8	1,383.6

Source: Direction de l'Artisanat

In Kenitra alone, it was said that eight years ago there were no large rug factories: now there are more than 30, each employing several hundreds of girls.

Many of the firms visited were companies with interests throughout Morocco. Many new factories were planned by the factory owners interviewed.

At the same time the Moroccan population is growing faster than its educational system and one and a half million girls do not attend primary school. These girls provide an obvious source of cheap labour to factory owners.

A decline in standards of rug-making was also clearly noticeable. Regional-style rugs are made anywhere in the country as well as in their reputed place of origin, officially stamped in the town of the head office of the firm, not where they are made, and shipped out in bulk. The tradition of the craftsman has been replaced by the mass-production factory.

An unpleasant feature of the rug-making scene is the use of an intermediary, the *maalema,* who recruits the girl workers herself and thus relieves the employer of all responsibility towards his workers (see next chapter). Another unpleasant feature is the contrast between the well-appointed head office of a rug factory and the dark, cramped, back street premises of its scattered workshops.

2. Child Workers, Maalema and Conditions

With Morocco's carpet industry booming and fortunes being made rapidly by the factory owners, child workers have an important place in the scheme of things. In only eight of the 62 private premises visited were little girls not actually seen at work — and three of these premises were head offices of companies which employed children elsewhere.

In 28 factories/workshops at least one-third of the employees were under 12, sometimes as many as three-fifths. These children were often only 8, 9 or 10 years old.

Hours were long: two factories visited worked a 72-hour week; five worked 60-64 hours a week. Half of those for which information was obtained exceeded the 48-hour legal maximum for a week's work for *adults*.

Wages were meagre, with so-called apprentices earning nothing. An annual holiday with pay — laid down by the law — was almost totally unknown.

In many of the factories visited the children looked undernourished and over-worked. While most factories and workshops had lavatories and running water, working conditions were often poor: bad lighting, absence or excess of air, crowded looms.

On a less industrialized scale, a few of the small rug-making workshops provided an agreeable contrast. Although employing young girls, they neverthe-less offered pleasant surroundings and a more friendly atmosphere than the large factories where several hundred girls would be under the strict control of older women or male overseers.

Government establishments too were characterized by their good working conditions. The premises were generally modern and well laid out. The 48-hour week was universally respected in the 14 establishments from which information was obtained. Indeed, a week of less than 40 hours was worked in four of these centres.

State wages were not high, but apprentices frequently got one or two dirhams a day.

More than half the working force of three state centres was made up of children under 12. In this respect the state does not abide by its own legislation, for even apprentices under 12 are illegal. Yet one centre said its apprentices could start as young as eight. In six other state centres a number of under 12s were seen while in seven there were no children under 12. Conditions were worst in the two centres using the *maalema* system.

The team tried to determine whether conditions had improved in those establishments mentioned in the first report. Certainly in one of them improvements had been made. Whether this was fortuitous or as a result of the team's visit was impossible to find out.

Two companies visited in 1975 now refuse entry to their workshops, in one of which conditions are extremely bad — as they evidently were then. The refusal of many employers to allow visitors to see the workshops is significant in this respect. There was no indication that the state work inspectors had been any more assiduous than before, despite the Moroccan government's statement of intent in January 1976.

It is clear that as long as primary school remains inaccessible to so many children, especially girls, this situation will continue (see Appendix A). It should not be forgotten, moreover, that thousands of Moroccan families are very poor and that these small girls' wages are an important element in their survival. Parents play into the hands of the factory owners in their desire to see their daughters bringing in even a small sum of money.

It should be remembered, too, that an adult working man's minimum legal wage is also very small. Furthermore, the exploitation of children is not limited to rug factories: small boys work long hours as apprentices in a number of crafts and trades and no legislation whatever exists to protect domestic help — often a child of 9 or 10.

Compulsory primary education would put an end to all this, but is obviously not feasible at present.

Working Methods and Pay

In general, a rug-making loom is worked by a team of four to eight girls. Larger looms — able to make rugs five metres wide — can accommodate more people, while it is not uncommon in smaller workshops to find a loom being worked by only one or two girls. One girl or woman is responsible for each loom.

The workers stand or sit on a bench, sometimes raised as the work progresses, knotting with one hand and cutting off the wool with a pair of scissors or a knife with the other. The rug's design is drawn on squared paper and stands beside each loom.

The girls work with great speed and dexterity. The amount each loom produces in a day depends of course on the number of workers, the complexity of the design, the thickness of the wool and the amount of beating given to each line of weft.* One square metre a day of simple design is about the maximum for a team of five or six.

The person responsible for each loom is sometimes an older girl or an ex-

---

*Lightly packed, "15/15", that is to say, 15 horizontal knots and 15 vertical knots per 10 sq.cm., or more thickly packed, "40/40" — 40 knots in each direction per 10 sq.cm.

perienced woman. However, there does exist in factories a system which is a relic of the old craftsman-apprentice structure. A qualified craftswoman, a *maalema,* supplies her own team and is paid for the work she produces. In turn, she pays her workers as she sees fit.

Originally, the *maalema* worked in her own home, with as many looms as she could manage but rarely exceeding three of four, with up to 20 workers. Many of her workers would be apprentices, waiting their turn to become *maalema* and set up on their own. Sometimes these unpaid apprentices were lodged, fed and clothed by the *maalema,* who might take a personal interest in their well-being. On other occasions the apprentices were little more than slaves — it all depended on the character of the *maalema.*

The transfer of this system to the factory is prejudicial to the children but convenient to the factory owners. The employer pays the *maalema* per square metre worked and has no further responsibility towards the children. He does not know who they are, how old they are, whether they stay one week or several years.

The *maalema* has every interest in squeezing the maximum amount of work out of her charges, to whom she pays the minimum possible rate. She has absolute control over these children and can recruit and discharge them as she likes.

In four of the big factories visited, *maalema* were responsible for engaging and paying the children. This was also the case in two government centres and in the majority of the smaller workshops. In three equally large factories it was said that the *maalema* system was definitely not used.

The wages paid by the employer to the *maalema* depend on the square metres worked by her team. In the four factories/workshops where information was obtained, the salaries ranged from 15 to 30DH a square metre, equivalent to one or two days' work. In the two state enterprises, 25DH was recorded.

Where the workers were paid a daily wage, this varied from 2DH to a maximum of 6DH, with the average around 4DH (women and girls). In only one establishment (Midelt) were the workers paid as much as 12DH a day.

"Apprentices" usually got nothing, or a maximum of one DH a day (a 500 gram loaf of bread costs 0.60DH). In one case apprentices had to bring presents to the factory manageress. Overtime working slightly increased the day's pay.

Some apprentices in state concerns got nothing. Others were paid 2 or 3DH a day. Qualified workers in state enterprises sometimes got as little as 2.50DH a day, sometimes as much as 5DH and once 200DH a month was noted. This is not taking into account those "true" cooperatives where the workers shared the profits.

3. Local Attitudes to Child Labour

Employers were generally reluctant to let visitors see working conditions in the factories or to discuss the children working for them. On many occasions entry to the loom area was strictly forbidden and doors firmly shut. There was an obvious desire not to draw attention either to the number of girls employed or to their ages.

Many factories were completely anonymous. This was particularly so of small workshops working for a large company. Hidden away in back streets or poor districts, they were only identified by the noise coming from them.

Two employers, however, spoke with warmth of the beneficial effects of their factories in supplying work to needy families. One employer of a smallish concern was said to be "like a father" to his workers. The overall impression was nevertheless one of indifference to the children. No employer was willing either to discuss the wages he paid his workers or how well off a *maalema* was compared to other salaried workers.

The companies had certainly no difficulty in finding children to work for them. Many factories were near *bidonvilles* (shanty towns) or in poor districts of the towns. One employer, however, did admit that if more schools continued to be built there would be a labour problem, as more and more children attended school.

For the moment there is no shortage of children to work in rug-factories and employers have the upper hand in a country where unemployment and under-employment are very high.

A Marrakesh *maalema* to whom the team spoke had a different story, however. According to her, young girls no longer wanted to go into the rug-making business. It was not that they preferred school but simply that they preferred doing nothing to working hard for a tiny wage.

Her story was supported by another group of Marrakesh rug-makers, who said there used to be 30 of them but that there were now only 11. On the whole, however, it was noted that there was no shortage of child labour.

Parents, too, were keen to see their daughters working. Some Agadir parents felt happy that their girls were "out of mischief" and under supervision. Another mother begged a small workshop to take on her child as she was "impossible" at home.

Some parents liked to inspect the premises where their daughters worked, but the majority were only too glad to have extra money coming into the house, even a few dirhams a day. A father spoken to said conditions where his two daughters worked were bad and the money poor, but it was obviously better than nothing.

In some of the smaller workshops seen, working conditions were undoubtedly better than in the children's home. This was invariably true in the state craft centres. In addition, families were pleased to have the girls learning a useful craft. As a generalization, Moroccan parents are ambitious for their sons but tend not to seek schooling for their daughters.

One father told the first team: "What use is school to a girl? She doesn't learn anything useful and she doesn't earn anything. She is expected to marry and that is her future".

The girls themselves often spoke with great freedom and frankness if given the chance, even inside some of the most factory-like of premises. It was easier, nevertheless, to talk to the children outside the factory.

One girl said she would not be doing the work if she could have been at school, while another said earning money was better than going to school. Many said the work was "good" and only one said it was hard. Most girls accept that they have to work hard in life.

The majority were reluctant to say how much they earned — except for apprentices who were eager to insist that they got nothing at all for their work. A few girls said the pay was "good".

In some premises visited, discipline was too severe to allow visitors to talk to the girls or even to see them at work. *Maalema* and male overseers were quick to reprimand idle, chattering girls. The workers in most establishments were light-hearted despite the poor conditions.

An inquiry into the family situation of a number of girls working in one rug factory revealed that in the majority of cases there were as many members of the family not working as working. In other words, the wages of the child worker — small as they were — were an important supplement to the family's resources.

The fathers of these children were generally employed, while the mother and younger brothers and sisters remained at home. Sometimes one or two elder brothers would be working and an equal number would be out of work, if only temporarily.

The situation of orphans or semi-orphans working in rug-making or embroidery workshops was said by many people to be disquietening. Cases were mentioned where the girls were virtually slaves, but no specific information concerning these cases was obtained.

4. Report on Factories and Workshops Visited

Agadir

Agadir is not a town particularly noted for its craft tradition, nor does its modern industry seem to affect this branch of activity. The tourist trade, however, provides a steady source of buyers of all types of craftwork. Only one rug-making establishment and one embroidery workshop were visited, both under the same ownership.

>   **Sud Artisanat**, 6 avenue Mouqaouama, Agadir. Telephone 32-70.
>   Owner: Mohamed Aguerouaz.
>   Founded: 1971 (K)*
>   Limited company (s.a.r.l.)
>   Capital 200,000DH (K)
>   Number of employees: 100
>   Turnover: 500,000-1,000,000DH (K)
>   Hours of work (44-hour week): 0800-1200 and 1400-1800 (shut Saturday
>   afternoon and Sunday).

The young owner of this rug-making concern and the embroidery workshop noted below was a man who had risen by his own efforts, and who had a genuine concern for his workers. He was "like a father" to them and it seemed that many families were pleased to have their daughters working for him, where "they would be out of mischief". It was said that he invested his capital to improve the business: for example, a concrete building recently replaced wooden sheds.

The rugs were exhibited in two large rooms looking on to a large patio. In a third room, 50 girls were at work on 42 looms; 18 of those seen were under 12. Normally the enterprise has some 100 workers. Some are "qualified", others are "apprentices". Many of the latter were aged from 8 to 11.

Some older children brought their young sisters and they were all better dressed than the children seen at SOCATAR and Tapis Berbères in Marrakesh, or in some of the Tangier and Tetuán workshops.

Conditions of work were excellent. Not only were there toilets, drinking

*K = Information from *Register of Moroccan Industry and Commerce "Kompass"*, 3rd edition, 1975/76.

14

water, a sickroom and a regular medical visit (the doctor was there on the morning of the team's visit), but Mr Aguerouaz arranged for the families of his workers to receive medical care, too.

He had also organized lessons in arithmetic and French, given by a paid visiting teacher during working hours. Girls attended these classes voluntarily and some two-thirds took advantage of these lessons.

At lunchtime and again in the evening a lorry collected the girls to take them home. Most girls went home to lunch. They could take an unpaid summer holiday.

There was no *maalema*. A girl said that the oldest among them were responsible for each loom. Another young girl trimming a rug said it was hers and was keen to sell it.

This establishment was among the best visited (though no information was available on wages), and was almost unique for its owner's attempts to educate and look after his workers.

Production: 600-1,000 square metres per month (100-200 rugs) exported to Germany, Sweden, Switzerland, France, the United States and sold on the local market.

Price: Plain 120DH/sq.m., Rabat: 327DH/sq.m.

Sud Artisanant, Broderie Mhabba, rue de Baghdad, Agadir. Telephone: 32-71.
Owner: Mohammed Aguerouaz
Number of employees: 30-40
Hours of work: (36-hour week) 0800-11.30 and 1400-1700 (shut Saturday afternoon and Sunday).

About 30-40 girls were embroidering in a large, sunny, well-lit room looking out on to a garden. They were under the strict but kindly eye of a European.

For nine to 12 months a girl was an apprentice and earned nothing. Then she sat an examination and became a qualified worker, paid by piecework. A good worker could earn 150DH a month and could, if she wished, take her embroidery away to work on at home.

The hours were short, it was explained, because the work was demanding and tiring for the eyes. The girls went on holiday with their families in the summer.

All styles of Moroccan embroidery were done, generally to order. The customers were largely Europeans.

Working conditions were very good, with wash basins and running water. Each worker sat at a desk, sometimes two to a desk.

Two girls were perhaps on the borderline of 11-12, the others were all older girls who had, in theory at least, completed some years of primary schooling. Apart from soft music from one girl's transistor radio, the room was in silence. All the girls went home to lunch.

Casablanca

This large industrial city, Morocco's economic capital, lies sixth in national production of hand-made rugs. The team visited five factories and one government school of apprenticeship.

In the Medina, however, there are several private houses in which some 15-20 children work regular hours for a *maalema,* who is the intervening agent between them and the factory owner. This is a situation that also occurs in Marrakesh. None of these small family-style workshops was visited.

REVISIT

CTIMA (Coopérative de Tissage Marocain), 20 rue de Sauternes. Tel: 435-22
Managing Director: Miloud Cuermoudi
Founded: 1952 (K)
Number of employees: 80-200 (300 according to previous report)
Hours of work: unknown, but shut Saturday afternoon and Sunday.

About 100 women and children were working in this well-lit (by electricity) well-aired factory. The premises carried the name CTIMA and were easy to find.

The room in which the rugs were being made was large and the looms well separated. A number of the children were well under 12. The imported wool came from the SAFT in Rabat (see page 38). The factory was shut for the month of August,

A little before 1800 hours the team saw a lorry collect the women and girls. Some 40 workers climbed in, 10 of whom were very young. General conditions looked good.

Production: 2,000 sq.m/month.
Styles: all kinds, including Moyen Atlas, Rabat and modern.
Prices : Plain — 180-200DH/sq.m., according to quality. Rabat — 350DH/sq.m. (30/30), Mediouna — 380DH/sq.m. (30/30).

REVISIT

Somafita (Société Marocaine de Filature et Tapis) Km 6,700 rue Oqba ben Nafia. Telephone: 443-49
Manager: Madame Fatima Herres
Founded 1972 (K)
Limited company (s.a.r.l.)
Number of employees: 120-150 (K)
Capital 30,000DH
Factory area: 800sq.m. under cover (K)
Hours of work: see previous report (shut Saturday afternoon and Sunday).

Two rugs hanging on a post on the pavement and a faded sign pointed out this establishment. The company seemed to have changed its premises slightly since the previous visit in 1975. SOMAFITA now occupied the first floor of a factory on the ground floor of which — entered by a separate door — was a welding plant making various types of machinery.

The present premises were well-aired and well-lit, with daylight coming in overhead and through translucent panels along one wall. In a large uncrowded room some 60 looms were noted, about half of them inactive.

There was an average of two to three girls per loom with sometimes as many as eight. Some 60-70 girls were counted, about one-third of them under 12. Behind a crowded loom some children were cooking their lunch.

There was a smell of urine from the toilets, which were nevertheless situated close to a small open-air balcony/terrace.

Conditions in this factory were good and far better than they must have been at the time of the first visit. The girls were not under close supervision. There was no summer holiday — in fact it is a period when most work is done and school-children on holiday come in to work. All rugs were to order and the wool was Moroccan.

Talking to three or four girls outside (working in spite of the Saturday afternoon) the team learned that they did 16 months' unpaid apprenticeship. During this period they said they even had to bring presents to Madame Herres. One said the work was hard and she would not be doing it if she could have been at school. Another walked 2 kilometres to get to the factory.

They said a *maalema* earned 18DH a square metre and they hoped that one day they would become a *maalema*. They said a German woman chose the designs and colours.

Production: 400-700 sq.m./month, according to Madame Herres, exported to Germany.

Styles: Moyen Atlas, Rabat.

Prices : plain: 140-155DH/sq.m. according to wool; Rabat: 300DH/sq.m.

REVISIT

Maroc Tapis, 94 boulevard Abdelmoumen, Derb Challef, Casablanca.

    Telephone: 590-88

Owner: Ahmed Jaidi

Number of employees: 23 seen at time of visit (60 in previous report)

Hours of work: all week except Sunday.

A fairly large, well-lit room housed a number of well-separated looms. Music was being played on a transistor radio. A pleasant Arabic-speaking woman was pleased to show visitors the rugs being made by the girls.

Of the 23 girls present, at least six were under age. One said she was 10.

The Moroccan woman said it took four weeks to make a square metre of Rabat rug and two weeks for a Moyen Atlas. The wool came from the SAFT in Rabat.

The number of girls to a loom varied from one to eight, with an average of four or five. One girl questioned as to what she earned would only say "not much — it depends on the work done during the week". The workers would seem to be paid on a piecework system. Another informant said that the girls were paid 4DH a day. The only *maalema* was the woman in charge.

17

This was one of the few establishments where the *Réglement de Travail* and *Accidents de Travail* — official regulations covering working conditions and accidents — were conspicuously pinned up (though it is doubtful if any of the girls could read). Conditions were certainly as good as in any factory visited and there was no feeling of the girls being repressed or over-disciplined.

This factory would seem to have improved since the last visit.

Production: unknown, but likely to be small and confined to the local market.
Prices (retail): Moyen Atlas 200DH/sq.m., Marmoucha 200DH/sq.m., Rabat 300DH/sq.m., Chinese 400DH/sq.m.

REVIST

Satiss, 5 rue de la Marine, ancienne Medina, Casablanca
Owner: A. ben Driss
Number of employees: 500 according to previous report
Hours of work: 0700-1900 probably with a lunchtime break (shut Saturday afternoon and Sunday).

A large metal doorway, clearly marked SATISS, led into a small room which in turn led into two offices, in one of which Mr ben Driss was working.

At a lower level could be seen a large workshop, tightly packed with looms and workers. There were at least 80 looms but it was difficult to calculate the number of girls since Mr ben Driss firmly shut the door of the workshop and said that entrance to it was strictly forbidden. However, it was possible to get some information on conditions on the shop floor.

There must have been several hundred girls since the team could see three to six sitting at each loom. A great many of them were under 12. The girls were unwilling to talk and were closely watched by a male overseer. However, one said she was paid 30DH for each metre she made.

Working conditions in this semi-basement looked particularly bad. There were no windows and the lighting was by electricity. The premises were stuffy and headache-inducing.

Mr ben Driss declared proudly that he supplied work to those children not attending school, to those no longer at school and to the handicapped.

Between 0730 and 0810 hours, 16 women and girls and 19 young children entered the premises by a door in the place de Belgique. The team assumed that work officially started at 0700, since these were the last to arrive.

In the evening, between 1800 and 1915 hours, 17 women and girls came out, together with 21 little girls. A further 67 women and 20 little girls came out between 1915 and 1945 hours. A total of 105 workers were thus counted, of whom a third were under 12.

However, the door was still open at 1945 hours and there were lights on in the building. Several dozen women went *into* the factory during this time and did not come out. It is possible that an evening shift was worked, but this is not certain.

*Production :*not known, but exported to Germany.
Styles: specialists in Moyen Atlas.
Prices: 160-180DH/sq.m.

AFRITAP, rue Adam (angle with rue de Tiznit, behind International Fair ground)
Owner: Mr Madrane

A dark ground-floor room housed the looms of this smallish concern. Mr Madrane's office and the finishing area were on the first floor, part of which was open to the sky.

Mr Madrane, who received visitors with great courtesy, said he had 21 looms. They were packed close together and there were about 50 girls at work, most of them aged between 14 and 16. The team noticed only four or five very young girls. The wool was imported duty-free (temporary importation).

A girl worker said that those girls who were apprenticed received no salary, while the qualified ones got 15DH a square metre. Apart from the rather crowded weaving room and its poor lighting (daylight, but dim), conditions were average and the girls seemed happy.

Production: 700-800 sq.m./month, exported to Germany.
Styles: especially Moyen Atlas.
Prices: Moyen Atlas (15/15) 160DH/sq.m.

Fez (Fés)

In both 1975 and 1976 Fez lay in third place for hand-knotted rug production, well behind Tangier and Rabat. It is also well-known for its embroidery. Official figures for 1975 indicated that there were 30,000 craftsmen and 15 craft co-operatives (all branches) in the town and that craft exports were steadily increasing.

The team visited seven rug-making concerns, one state embroidery cooperative and one state craft centre.

REVISIT

Makina, bab de Kaken, Grand Mechouar, BP23, Fez. Telephone: 349-50
Directors: Jean Victor Cherpin, Jean Louis Thau, Emile Capdevieille
Limited company (s.a.) (K)
Number of employees: 250 (K) but see below
Hours of work (60-hour week): 0700-1200 and 1300-1800 (shut Sunday).

It was explained at the door that this was a private company and that as individual orders were no longer taken, entry had been refused to visitors for the last seven months. Many outside informants said that entry to this factory had in fact been refused following publication of a very unfavourable report in the daily newspaper *L'Opinion* in about July or August 1976.*

*This article was not traced, despite much searching in the Bibliothèque Générale.

Two girl workers spoken to as they went in confirmed the report of the previous team that 1,000 women and children worked in this factory. They said they ate their lunch on the premises and had a month's summer holiday with "a little" money. They said that the *grand patron* (employer) paid the *maalema* and she paid her workers.

There were girls of all ages, starting at 7. They agreed that most of the apprentices were very young, but were reluctant to lose more time talking, so no further information was available.

By all accounts, this factory still continues to employ young children for very long hours in very bad conditions (see photographs).

Production: all exported.
Styles: Moyen Atlas, Rabat, Persian.

Fes Tapis, Douh Derb Sekalia, 1, Boujeloud, Fez
Owner: Abdelkrim Ouadrari
Hours of work (72-hour week): 0700-1900 (shut Sunday).

Mr Ouadrari said he had four rug factories in Fez, with 34 looms in the one visited and somewhat fewer in each of the others.

The premises were windowless and lit by neon lighting. Between 200 and 300 girls were seen at work, though there could have been more in this very crowded room. A great many of these girls were very young, perhaps 9 or 10 years old.

The wool was imported ready spun from France.

There was no summer holiday and working conditions were generally bad although Mr Ouadrari and his staff were pleasant and helpful. The hours worked here were exceptionally long.

Production: 3,000 sq.m./month, exported to Germany.
Styles: Moyen Atlas (15/15).
Price: 150DH/sq.m.

Société Fassi de Tissage (SO.FA.TI), 13/15 rue 206, Ain Kadours, Fez.
Telephone: 336-02.
Directors: Mr Idrissi and Abderrahman Touzani
Hours of work: unknown but shut Sunday

This was the only rug-making factory owned by the company, although they had a dyeing establishment in Fez for their wool, which was imported, ready-spun from France. They had just moved to this part of Fez and were occupying the premises noted in the telephone directory as Tapis Saada (Lasrak Hadj Mohammed and Serhane Driss).

There were said to be 50 looms and 200 girls in the factory, but only 23 girls were actually at work at the time of the visit. Among them were three or four very young workers. The looms were well separated and there was a toilet and running water. Conditions were generally average and the staff helpful. There were no *maalema*.

Production: 1,000 sq.m./month, made to order, exported to Germany.

Styles: only Moyen Atlas (15/15 and 16/16).
Prices: Moyen Atlas 140-210DH/sq.m. according to quality and design.

Africtapis, 31 rue el Hammam, Ain Kadous Fez.
Owner: Morocco Carpet, Rabat (Zniber family) see pages 29, 32 and 33.

A blank metal doorway led into this crowded factory. The first room was dark and windoweless, the second rather better lit. There were said to be 50 looms and they were tightly packed together. About 150 girls were seen at work, including at least half under 12

Production: figures available only from head office.
Styles: limited to Moyen Atlas.

Société Zerhouni-Filati-Ansari "Les Doigts Magiques", 31, Ain Harouh, Quartier El Farah, Zanka 210, Fez.

This factory prided itself on its "extra-superior" quality and the work was certainly of a high standard. There were said to be 50 girls and 20 looms on the premises. Five other looms had been given to workers who had married and these women produced work in their own homes.
Several small girls were at work. The room had windows but was rather dark. The male staff in charge were helpful and proud of their high-quality work. Conditions seemed average.

Production: 100 sq.m./month, for local wholesale merchants.
Styles: Moyen Atlas, Persian (40/40) and Rabat (30/30).
Prices: Rabat 150-300DH/sq.m., Moyen Atlas 120-200DH/sq.m.

Tapis Anowar, Mekouar et Ben Lamlil, Bab Sifer, R.3, 13, Ain Haroun, Fez.
Manager: Mr Mekouar
Hours of work (72-hour week): 0700-1900 (shut Sunday).

These premises displayed no name and little information was available since the manager was busy in the upstairs office. A male employee said there was no mid-day break.
At least 100 girls were at work in a large room, many of them under 12. The looms were packed close together and the light from the small windows had to be supplemented by electricity. The ceiling was very low and the workshop stuffy. Conditions looked poor and the hours worked were excessive.

Styles: Rabat and Persian.

Houari Lazrak, 6 place de l'Istiqlal, Batha, Fez.
Hours of work (51-hour week): 0700-1200 and 1430-1800 (shut Friday)

Mr Lazrak's factory was shut on the day of the visit. A neighbouring shopkeeper said "many" women and girls worked there, some of them very young indeed. It was not possible to make a personal visit to confirm this information.

21

Kenitra

This large modern town and port only became important relatively recently, but it is now one of the most increasingly industrialized towns of Morocco. It is the fifth most important town for rug production and two factories were visited, as well as the government craft centre.

> Société Artisanale de tissage de tapis (SAAT), 132 boulevard Moulay Youssef (factory), Kenitra. Owner: Haj Thami Lyazghai. Telephone 38-40.
> Retail Shop: Au Progrès Artisanl, 91, avenue Mohamed Diouri, Kenitra.
> Number of employees: 400
> Hours of work (54-hour week): 0800-1200 and 1400-1900 (shut Sunday).

This factory was clearly identified and easy to find. A large room, well-lit with overhead daylight and high roof, contained some 60-70 looms, packed close together. There were three to eight girls per loom. A total of 182 women and children were counted and at least three-fifths were under 12. Many were said to be only 6, 7 or 8 years old.

There was a certain amount of dust but conditions, though factory-style, were otherwise reasonable. The girls sang at their work and were ready to talk. Discipline did not seem too strict, although the girls worked with great rapidity.

There was no summer holiday: the girls could go off — they were "easily replaceable". Only a few male workers were regular employees and received steady wages. The girls were taken on by the *maalema* responsible for each loom, and she paid them as she thought fit. She herself was paid an unknown sum per square metre.

One girl said in French that she was "well paid". Another informant said the older girls were paid 5-6DH a day.

The owner, Mr Lyazghai, was vice-president of the Chambre de Commerce Artisanale in Rabat. He was pleased to show off his factory and said he had three others, each of the same size, and employed a total of 1,400-1,500 workers,* with 260 looms.

He had started eight years ago when there were no such factories in Kenitra. Now there were 30 other rug-making concerns in the town, all as important as his. He imported his wool from France (12 tons per month and four to five tons of cotton). He said he had just received an order for 500,000 square metres from West Germany and had orders that would take him up to the end of the year.

Haj Lyazghai explained that Moroccan carpets were now the best for quality and price and that the Moroccan government was very helpful towards rug-manufacturers. For instance, they were exempt from import duty on looms and wool (the latter imported under "temporary" licence for re-exportation) and from export duty on the finished articles and from certain taxes.

He felt that factories such as his did a lot of good for the country and were particularly beneficial in bringing work to the region. He said that low labour

*On the basis of the three-fifths under 12 seen here, this would mean a total of about 900 under-age children employed by the SATT.

costs were instrumental in making Moroccan carpets highly competitve in the European market, "where trade unions and high wages make such an activity impossible".

Production: 5,000 sq.m./month (this factory), exported to France ("Le Printemps"), Great Britain and West Germany.
Price: Moyen Atlas 150DH/sq.m., Rabat 350DH/sq.m.

Manufacture de Tapis Marocains, 14, rue 9, Quartier Rabada, Kenitra
Owner: Mr Omari (Algerian)
Hours of work: (48-hour week) 0800-1200 and 1400-1600 (shut Sunday).

The entrance to this factory was through a large metal gate opened only on request. On the ground floor, in a not very large room, 44 looms were packed very closely together, with two to five girls per loom. About 100 workers were counted, some of them women, but at least 50 were very small girls aged 6, 7 and 8.

There was no annual holiday: "If the girls want to take a holiday, there is nothing stopping them". The premises lacked air but there was a toilet.

It took five to six days to make a 6 square metre rug. There was a *maalema* in charge, aged about 30, and she said a worker who was responsible for a loom could earn up to 500DH a month. No other information was available on salaries or method of engaging workers.*

Production: 50-60 packages, representing 600 sq.m., exported to Germany and Great Britain each month.
Styles: traditional and modern.
Prices: modern 150DH/sq.m.

Marrakesh

In 1973, Marrakesh was fourth in the list of rug-producing cities. By 1976 it had dropped to fifth. Despite this decline, rug-making continues to be an important craft activity in a city which is the least industrialized of any large Moroccan town (less than one factory worker for seven craftsmen).

According to 1971 figures, some 5,000 female workers were engaged in craft-work, mainly in textiles and clothing. In 1977, official sources gave the total number of workshops engaged in rug-making (excluding work in private houses) as 116 for the Nord, Centre, Sud, Bab Doukkala and Sidi Youssef ben Ali districts of the city.

It is characteristic of the Marrakesh area that craft establishments of all types are small (figures for 1972): 93.25% of them had under 10 workers (64% of the labour force); 4.75% had 10-49 workers (16% of the labour force) and only 2% had more than 50 workers (20% of the labour force).

*On the basis of the square metre per day indicated, a month of 26 working days would produce 26 sq.m. and the loom leader would accordingly be paid at the rate of about 20DH a square metre.

Information was obtained from two establishments in Marrakesh that could be called industrial, from one large workshop and from eight small family-type concerns. In addition, a third industrial establishment was noted in the city and a fourth visited in a village some 100 kilometres west of Marrakesh. Two government weaving centres were also visited, one in Marrakesh and one in Chichaoua, 77 kilometres west of Marrakesh.

Société Marrakech Tapis – Manufacture de Tapis Berbères, 10, rue Fatima ez Zohra (near Dar Si Said), Marraskesh. Telephone: 238-24, 238-27.

Owner: Mr Genfoud, an Algerian working in association with the Algerian owner of SOCATAR (information from Chambre d'Artisanat, Marrakesh).

Entry to this establishment was refused by the Moroccan who answered the door and who quickly shut it again. Beyond the slightly opened metal gates a loom could be seen standing in a darkish room, dimly lit by light coming in from high above. From time to time a small girl came in or out but none would speak.

By waiting outside this factory from 0720 to 0805 one morning, it was possible to see the workers arriving. About a quarter of them arrived together at 0730. Some 66 girls over 14 were counted, together with 104 very small girls, many of whom looked about 7, 8 or 9 years old.

Each arrived with a little packet, probably lunch. A few were accompanied by a mother, or by a brother on a bicycle. All the smaller girls were very poorly dressed. The gates shut at 0805. No other information was available.

SOCATAR (Société Atlas Artisanale), 59, rue des Domaines (near Palais de la Bahia).

There was nothing on the metal gates to identify this establishment. The team was refused entry. However, the Moroccan who answered the door provided some information.

He said about 420 girls worked in this factory. Production was 4,000, 5,000 or even 6,000 square metres per month, with contracts said to be for 20 years ahead.

The rugs were made to order and were of modern design. The wool was imported from France and the finished articles sent to the head office in Dunkirk, France, from where they were dispatched mostly to West Germany. The employee said there was no office in Marrakesh.

An open-air courtyard could just be seen, with some looms and a few girls in a room on the far side. A high wall enclosed the premises, which looked as though they could well contain 400 workers.

Waiting outside one evening, the team was able to count the workers as they came out after work. Between 1758 and 1845 hours, 143 women and girls emerged: 13 were probably *maalema,* 41 were girls over 12 and 89 were girls under 12. The team noted that nearly all had empty shopping baskets, which may have contained their lunch. No information was available on hours of work.

The Direction de l'Artisanat in Marrakesh, said that SOCATAR had an office in Marrakesh, at 38 boulevard Mohamed Zerktouni, Guéliz, and that the owner was an Algerian. At this address, outside in the street, a man said the owner was called Si Abdelkader and he had girls working in three carpet factories in Marrakesh. (This was unconfirmed, and no further information was obtainable from the Direction de l'Artisanat.)

Fabrique Aherdane, Quartier Industrial, Marrakesh (near College Ibn Toumert).

This establishment, said to employ many women and girls working in shifts, was shut for a spring holiday at the time of the visit. No further information was available.

Tapis Mabrouka, Riad ben Nacer, Ank Jmal Riad Laross, Marrakesh.
Telephone: 329-39.
Number of employees: 20-25
Hours of work: 8 hours a day (shut Sunday) (48-hour week).

The owner, a pleasant young French-speaking Moroccan woman, was happy to show off her establishment and spoke of it with enthusiasm.

A traditional Moroccan house, with garden and courtyard, had recently (March 1976) been converted into a workshop. Conditions were excellent: two rectangular rooms, looking on to a large sunlit courtyard, housed five looms each. In another room a number of girls, all over 12, were doing embroidery.

Only three rug-makers were seen on the premises, but the owner said some 15-20 girls were absent at that moment. Two of the girls seen may have been under 12, but a photograph of the owner surrounded by 12 girls did not include any under 12.

The owner said she paid her employees 2-3DH a square metre. (Two small girls seen just outside on leaving said they earned nothing, but it was not absolutely certain they really worked there). This wage seems extraordinarily low and perhaps referred to a daily wage.

Apart from these very low wages, the establishment gave an excellent impression. There was no feeling of strict discipline and the children seemed happy and were working with plenty of light and air. Conditions were probably far better than in their own homes.

Prices: plain white: 150DH/sq.m., with pattern: 170DH/sq.m.

Other Weaving Workshops

A feature of the rug-making industry in Marrakesh was the number of small workshops with one to four looms and from four to 15 employees. The looms were sometimes on shop premises, sometimes in private houses. In the latter case it was not easy to distinguish them from genuinely family affairs. A certain number of these small workshops were visited.

Bazaar in the Marché Berbère (near Dar Si Said and beside a bank)

One loom with five girls, all over 12, was in a darkish corner of the shop. The girls worked a square metre in three days but no information was available on hours of work.

Average prices (retail): 160DH/sq.m.

16, rue Derb el Bahia (near Dar Si Said)

One loom with eight girls, two under 12, was squeezed into a corner of a shop. The shop was popular with tourists. The eight workers took at least two, sometimes three to six days to finish a square metre, depending on complexity of design. Apart from a good toilet, conditions were poor. There was no fresh air and lighting was by electricity. The hours of work were 0800-1200 and 1400-1800, though the cashier said with great frankness that if they had orders to fulfil they doubled the hours.

La Porte du Sahara, 25-27, rue el Mouassine. Telephone: 220-79.
Owner: Moulay Abdallah Rafiai Idrissi

On the first floor, above the shop, two men were weaving blankets on a loom, a boy was working leather and one woman and two girls (aged 11-12) were making a rug. The rug-makers worked an eight-hour day for a salary of 3-4DH a day, with the *maalema* getting 18-20DH a square metre.

The owner said that one woman and four young girls could make a plain, 6 square metre rug in 10 days (sale price of rug 800DH) and a similar one more closely knotted in 15 days (sale price 1,000DH). Rugs with a pattern cost 1,200DH.

Working conditions were bad. There was little air and no light apart from electricity and the roof sloped down just above the heads of the rug-makers.

Bazaar opposite Post Office and beside Cercle de Rehamna (near Dar Si Said)

There was one loom in this large bazaar, somewhat dark but not cramped. One woman and three girls (one of whom was only about 7 or 8 years old) were weaving a rug but would not speak to visitors. No information was available.

Charia Houman el Ftouaki, Sidi Youssef ben Ali

In a private house, eight girls, at least three under 12, were working by electric light (in mid-afternoon) in a dark room looking on to a small courtyard. They said they were all one family.

Hours of work were rigid: 0700-1200 and 1400-1800 (a nine-hour day). They said they worked for Mr Genfoud (see page 24) and were paid "a little" money. They were working on a Sunday, but they may have had Friday off.

Douar Ain Itti

In a private house in this very poor district of Marrakesh 11 girls were working on a rug. A young *maalema* of 17 explained that there used to be 30 workers but that the figure had dropped recently.

The workers were from three families. They worked all day but not Friday and had one month's holiday in the summer (unpaid). They worked for Dar Si Said (the state craft cooperative). The *maalema* had been trained there and the designs for the rugs were supplied by Dar Si Said.

They were able to make all kinds of rugs and the *maalema* said she was paid "a little" for her work. The room was small and badly lit. One child was only 6 years old.

Douar Graoua, Derb lalla chaicha (beside Dar Si Said)

In a large warehouse-like room, well-aired and lit by daylight from the open air courtyard and overhead windows, eight girls (three under 12) were working a large loom. The *maalema* was absent and the girls spoke with ease.

They worked 0730-1200 and 1430-1900, with Friday off (54-hour week). They had 25 days' unpaid holiday in the summer.

The very young girls, "apprentices", were paid one DH a day, rising to 2DH for the qualified workers. They were paid by the *maalema* and did not know what happened to the finished work, but they knew some of it went to the Ensemble Artisanal (see page 49). The only water visible was in a large can.

Sidi Youssef ben Ali

Four looms were crammed in a dark, airless room of a private house in this poor quarter of Marrakesh. Fifteen girls were present, four of them very young. One girl was washing the cement floor.

The *maalema* was distrustful and disinclined to talk. The girls worked all week except Friday and could take a holiday in summer "if they liked" (unpaid). The *maalema* worked to order (probably in association with a bazaar owner). She received 130DH per square metre for her rugs, some of which could be seen on the premises.

One girl spoke a little French but the rest were subdued and silent. Working conditions were bad — the worse seen in this group.

Sidi Moktar (province of Marrakesh), 100 kilometres west of Marrakesh on road to Essaouira

This large village (2,741 inhabitants in 1960) is well-known for its rug-weavers and wool dyers.

Beside the dyers' workshops could be seen a high wall with a large anonymous metal gate. This was said by a local informant to be a new rug factory, the property of an Algerian living for 30 years in Tangier, who had another factory in the Guéliz district of Marrakesh (probably Si Abdelkader of SOCATAR).*

The informant did not know the name of the owner, but knew that he had asked for 350 workers, although only 90 women and children were actually working in this factory. The wool came from Tangier and all the rugs were for export. He said the gates were opened at 0700 and shut an hour later. The children went home for lunch, "not like the girls in the Marrakesh factory", and then worked from 1400 to 1830. There was said to be no summer break.

Waiting outside this factory from 1245 to 1320 hours it was possible to form an idea of the number and age of the employees. The first small girl came out at 1310, then a few minutes later whole batches appeared. At 1320 a man left after shutting the gate behind him.

The team counted 94 girls, of whom a half to two-thirds appeared to be under 12 (47-58). A few of the older girls were in *jellabas,* the rest were very simply dressed. Hours of work were probably 0700 to 1300 and 1400 to 1830 (a 63-hour week).

Meknès

In 1976 Meknès was seventh in the production of hand-made rugs. Meknès is also well-known for its embroidery.

As the city becomes increasingly industrialized, it is not surprising to find at least two factory-style rug-making concerns one a branch of a Rabat firm. In addition, five smaller private rug-making and embroidery work-shops were visited and two government centres.

Matima, 209, avenue de Jerusalem, Meknes-Riad. Telephone: 309-46
Managing Director: Mr Bouayad
Hours of work (48-hour week): 0800-1200 and 1400-1800 (shut Sunday).

The large, ornate but anonymous door of this factory was kept locked. Inside, a large finishing room was well lit, but a parallel room housing the looms was extremely dark. There appeared to be neither windows nor electric lighting.

A helpful employee said there were 80 looms. There could well have been some 200-300 girls at work, since they sat at least three or four to a loom. Many of the girls seen were under 12.

There was a toilet and running water. The factory was open all the year round. The wool was imported from France and it took two days to work one square metre of simple design.

Production: 4,000 sq.m./month, exported to Germany.
Styles: Moyen Atlas (15/15 and 20/20).
Prices: not available at time of visit.

Laines du Maroc, 8, Derb Hammam Moulay Ismael (near place Lalla Aouda), Meknès

*The International Carpet Factory in Tangier (see page 39) said that this Sidi Moktar factory was owned by the brother of Mr Boumédienne, himself the managing director of the International Carpet Factory.

This factory was difficult to find, since it was sited beyond several narrow passages. In a fairly large room several hundred girls were at work, some in their teens, many of them under 12. The room was congested and it was not possible to count the number of looms. It was, however, well lit with overhead daylight. The wool was Moroccan.

The head office of the factory was in Rabat (see page 33) and a hostile member of staff telephoned Mr Zniber in Rabat for information on prices. Mr Zniber himself said over the telephone that the company was not interested in further orders, being fully booked up for the next two years.

"Mhabba", Sahrij Souani (in old stables of Moulay Ismael, near Agdal), Meknès. Telephone: 303-39.
Owner: Mohamed Aguerouaz (see Agadir, page 15).
Number of employees: 50
Hours of work (44-hour week): 0800-1200 and 1400-1800 (shut Saturday afternoon and Sunday).

The rugs made in this workshop were sent to Mr Aguerouaz in Agadir, from where they were mainly exported. The workshop used to be owned by a European and a speciality was tapestry work of modern design. The work was of a very high standard and the girls were said to be all highly expert. No apprentices were hired.

Nineteen looms were seen in the seven one-time stables, and 29 girls were at work. Of these, only two were very young. The rest were all girls in their late teens. A small boy was also playing around and the two small girls may have been younger sisters.

The workrooms looked on to a large and pleasant garden and were well lit and well aired, being open to the garden in front. But they were said to be rather cold and damp in winter.

There was running water and a paid holiday was given in the summer. Conditions were generally good and it was agreeable to find an almost total absence of young children at work. The atmosphere was one of a skilled workshop rather than a factory.

Production: figures not available.
Styles: tapestry, Moyen Atlas and Rabat.
Prices (retail): Moyen Atlas 350DH/sq.m., Rabat 450DH/sq.m. All tapestry work: 700DH/sq.m.

Mme. Amina Aherdan, 11, Ferhat Hachad, Meknès. Telephone: 230-10
Owner: Mme. Amina Aherdan
Five rooms and an office in the grounds of a private house formed this rug-making, embroidery and sewing establishment. Fifteen embroiderers were seen at work (all over 12), although there were said to be 30. The room was well lit and music came from a transistor radio.

Six men were sewing *kaftans* in another room and two further rooms, rather darker, housed three looms, one of which was inactive.

In one of the rooms a middle-aged woman was working with nine children. In the other, one middle aged *maaalema* sat with six children. Of the 15 children seen, at least eight were aged 9, 10 or 11.

It was explained that the *maalema* was paid for her work and she recruited as many children as she liked — this was not Madame Aherdan's responsibility. The establishment was shut in August. Work was made to order.

Styles (rugs): Moyen Atlas.
Prices: not available at time of visit.

Derb Zemmouri, Medina, Meknès

In one room of this private house three girls were working at a loom. A second loom was idle. In another room several girls were sewing. None of the girls present at the time of the visit was under 12. They came in to work each day and said it took 15 days to do a square metre of Rabat rug. It was said that they worked for a bazaar owner.

Prices: Rabat (30/30) 250DH/sq.m.

Fatima Lamrabet, 44 Bab Gnaoua, Akkbat Ziadine, Meknès (behind Medina Post Office)

This embroidery workshop was pointed out as employing several girls, including young ones. Information on prices was given by three women in the small office but it was impossible to see the workshop and confirm the information that small girls were employed.

Private flat, above dentist, opposite CTM bus station, Medina, Meknès

Neighbouring shopkeepers said that this private flat is a place to which many young girls go to do embroidery work. The owner was said to have orders from outside Meknès, even from Fez.

However, an elderly and suspicious man inside said that only his own daughters and "a few friends of theirs" worked on the premises. He was willing to show what they made but not to allow visitors in.

*   *   *

(Despite much searching, the "Artisanat des Petites Filles" in the Medina of Meknès, mentioned in the previous report, was not found. In the absence of any address, or any indication of the area, the team had to rely on asking people. But no one was able to indicate where this house might be. There is no reason to suppose, however, that it does not still exist and flourish.)

Midelt

Midelt is a small country town on one of the main north-south routes across the Middle Atlas Mountains. The main activities of the region are mining and agriculture (especially the raising of large flocks of sheep and goats). Rugs and clothing have always been made by the local women for their personal use, but there is no particular tradition of craftwork nor any modern textile industry. The team visited one private rug-making and embroidery workshop.

Kasba Myriem, route de Jaffar, Midelt

Number of employees: 25 spinners, 45 weavers, 25 embroiderers — all women or girls over 14.

Hours of work (40-hour week): 0800-1145, and 1330-1745 (shut Friday and Sunday).

This establishment is run by a community of Franciscan nuns. It aims to provide employment at a decent level of remuneration for a number of local women. No children are employed.

The spinners call once a fortnight to receive a quantity of raw wool or to return wool they have spun at home. They are paid at present at a rate of 10-12DH for every kilogram spun. This is good payment compared with Casablanca, for instance, where some self-employed spinners work for as little as 3DH a kilo.

Conditions of work for the weavers and embroiderers are excellent: the premises are spacious, well-aired, well-lit, with windows opening on to a large garden/courtyard. In winter the room is heated, since temperatures can fall to below zero. Washing facilities and drinking water are provided. There is a three-week paid holiday in summer.

An average of four women and two or three apprentices sit at each loom, which are well separated from each other. The embroiderers sit on benches in the middle of the room.

All the trained women receive 12DH each a day, the apprentices 5-8DH a day. The apprentices spend half a day in the workshop and half a day in a class-room on the premises learning domestic subjects.

The *maalema* system did not operate here, all the workers being supervised by the nun in charge.

The economic success of this workshop is proof that it is possible to run a craftwork business — weaving or embroidery — without employing small children. Prices are higher than many commercial firms but good wages are paid.

Production: very difficult to estimate, due to the variety of work undertaken, but possibly about an average of 50 sq.m./month; on sale to visitors, both Moroccan and European.

Prices: about 250DH/sq.m. for the rugs, the embroidery varying according to the work involved.

Ouezzane

Ouezzane is situated some 130 kilometres north of Fez, on the road to Tetuán. It has a certain reputation for cloth-weaving. One private enterprise and one state cooperative were visited.

Anonymous workshop, place Si Rmel, near Lycée Moulay Abdallah Cherif, Ouzzane.

Working for Manufacture Rachidi of Tangier (see page 42).

Nothing indicated the existence of this workshop. Behind a large, locked wooden door were three dark, windowless rooms and a small open courtyard. In one small room were the finished rugs, in another some 25-30 girls were making them. The 34 looms were very close together and it was difficult to see. Half of the girls were clearly under 12.

There was no *maalema* and the man in charge was reluctant to talk, although it was possible to look around. Only the name Rachidi on the label gave a clue as to the destination of the work.

There were toilets and running water in the courtyard but otherwise conditions were bad. The locked door was an expressive sign of the atmosphere of this workshop.

Price: (retail) plain white: 210DH/sq.m. Finished rugs sent to Tangier.

Chechaouen

This town of some 15,000 inhabitants, lying halfway between Ouezzane and Tetuán, attracts a great number of tourists, and a correspondingly increasing number of bazaars sell all kinds of handicrafts. One state cooperative and one family-style weaving workshop were visited.

Dar Zrabi, down a street not far from the Parador Hotel, Chechaouen
Hours of work (48-hour week): 0800-1200 and 1400-1800 (shut one day a week).

Seven girls were working two looms in this private house. One looked about 10 years old but another girl affirmed that she was in fact 12. No information was available on wages, nor about for whom they worked, but the presence of a regular timetable for work would seem to indicate that this was not a purely family affair. The room was small and badly lit.

Rabat-Salé

According to figures published by the Direction de l'Artisanat, Rabat, capital of Morocco, produces by far the greatest amount of hand-made Moroccan rugs — more than double its nearest rival, Tangier. The ornate Rabat rug is an obvious speciality, but in fact rugs of all styles are made in this increasingly industrialized city and in its satellite the other side of the Bou Regreg River, Salé.

Eight industrial enterprises were visited (one featuring in the previous report) and one government cooperative (also in the previous report).

Société Morocco Carpet, 16, rue Omar Jdidi, Rabat (head office) Telephone: 349-01.
Managing Director: Mohamed Zniber. Director Abdelhadi Zniber (son)
Founded: 1968 (K)
Limited company (s.a.r.l.) 300,000DH (K)
Turnover: 5,000,000-10,000,000DH (K)
Number of employees: 600-700 (all factories) (K)

Hours of work (44-hour week): Rabat — 0800-1200 and 1400-1800 (shut Saturday afternoon and Sunday).

The main activity of this large company is the making of Moroccan hand-knotted rugs, but it also has a factory for the spinning and dyeing of rug wool. The raw rug wool is imported from West Germany.

The factory in Rabat was visited (route de Casa, Km.3, telephone: 301-01). The company also has factories in Salé (rue de la Convalescence, telephone: 382-80) and Fez (rue el Hammam Ain Kadous).

Several hundred women and girls were at work in a large room. An employee said there were 127 looms in this factory, with four or sometimes seven workers to a loom, but it was impossible to count the girls due to the very crowded conditions. Each of the other two factories has 130 looms.

There could well have been 500 girls present in the factories of Rabat. A glance revealed a great many under 12. It was explained that the *maalema* system operated in this factory, the girls being taken on and paid by a woman responsible for each loom. These girls were not known to the management.

Some of the girls went home at mid-day, others ate on the premises. Lorries collected them in the morning and evening.

Conditions were average for a factory: the premises were large, well-lit with daylight, the looms were very close together and there was a certain amount of dust. The staff was extremely amiable and the girls seemed happy.

Production: (this factory) 5,000 sq.m./month, exported to West Germany and Belgium.

Styles: Moyen Atlas (quality 15/15).

Prices: not available at the factory.

Laines du Maroc (beside the river between Rabat and Salé). Telephone: 388-97 and 383-85.

This enormous factory site was also under the management of the Zniber family (see above). However, it is not certain that it is the Salé factory listed, since an employee in the office said the address was "the old route de Rabat-Salé".

No workers were seen — it was in fact lunchtime — and entry to the factory was strictly forbidden. An empty lorry for collecting staff was seen outside.

No further information was obtained about this factory, except that an outside informant said that a number of girls had given up working there because conditions were very bad. It was also said that a great many women and children were employed. The company also had a factory in Meknés (see page 28).

El Haj Ahmed Bouchouari and Mohamed Bouchouari, boulevard de l'Oued, Salé. Telephone: 814-98.
Owners: the Bouchouari brothers
Number of employees: estimated 240-420
Hours of work (54-hour week): 0700-1200 and 1400-1800 (shut Friday).

Inside this unnamed factory and at the far end of a large open courtyard was a shed packed with girls and looms. The ceiling was low and one side of the room was partially open, allowing good ventilation in the spring and summer but undoubtedly cold and wet in winter.

The line of looms and girls continued down one side of the courtyard, hidden from view. There were toilet facilities and a lorry for transporting staff. Otherwise working conditions were very bad in these make-shift premises.

A friend of the owner said there 60 looms. Four to seven girls were noted at every loom, giving a total of between 240 and 420 girls on the premises. Many of them were well under 12.

The wool was Moroccan and came ready spun from FILROC, although the company did some of its own dyeing. An employee said there was no summer holiday.

Production: 4,000 sq.m./month, exported mainly to West Germany.
Styles: especially Moyen Atlas, but all kinds.
Prices: Moyen Atlas (quality 15/15) 130-150DH/sq.m.

13 Bab Sebta, Fondouk Aktouane, Medina, Salé

Neighbouring craftsmen pointed out this entirely anonymous establishment as being a rug-making concern. A young Moroccan who opened the blue-painted door said it was only the workshop and the owner was Sidi Ahmed Rahali, of Fabrica Berberia in Rabat. This turned out to be Berbère Carpet, 329 avenue Mohamed V. A secretary said the firm had workshops in Rabat and Salé.

Thirty looms were counted in this very crowded, low-roofed room, though there could well have been double that number. At least 120 girls were counted, the great majority very young.

It was lit by daylight overhead but conditions were otherwise bad. There are probably other workshops like this one hidden away in the Medina of Salé.

Manufacture de Tapis Marocain, 33, Bab Fes, Salé. Telephone: 386-46.
Owner: Mohamed Berrada
Hours of work (51-hour week): 0800-1200 and 1400-1830 (shut Sunday).

A very large, very high room held 50 looms, 35 of them in use. The room was well-lit by central overhead windows. The looms were wide apart and the premises were clean and airy. There was a toilet and running water.

Twenty-five girls were on the premises, but it was said that the others were still at lunch. A few of those seen were under 12.

A pleasant employee was happy to let visitors wander among the looms, though there was a notice saying "filming forbidden". The factory's wool came from FILROC (see page 38) and SAFT.

Production: not available.
Styles: all kinds, including Moyen Atlas, Rabat, Chichaoua, etc.
Prices: Moyen Atlas 240DH/sq.m., Rabat and Chichaoua (30/30) 300DH/ sq.m.

FITAM (Filature Tapis Marocain), Tabriquet, Salé. Telephone: 383-84
Managing Director: Zine Bernoussi
          Director: Tahar Sbai
Founded: 1973 (K).
Limited company (s.a.) 600,000DH (K)
Number of employees: 500-700 (K)

This large factory was conveniently placed near one large *bidonville* (shanty town) and one small one in a peripheral quarter of Salé.

A number of men and women were finishing rugs in one large room, while another very big room was closely packed with looms and girls. Four hundred girls were counted, but there could have been 560-840 since they sat three to eight to a loom. The team counted 140 looms (225 according to *Kompass).* Many of the girls were well under 12.

The centre of the room was well-lit with daylight overhead but the sides were badly lit. There were toilet facilities and a lorry to transport staff. The atmosphere was cheerful. An old man sitting outside said the girls earned 4 or 5DH a day.

Production: 4,000 sq.m./month, exported to Germany.
Styles: Moyen Atlas.
Prices: 170-240DH sq.m., according to quality.

Ets. Lanke – Tapis, Filature, Tissage, ancienne Gare de Salé-Bled, BP 168.
    Telephone: 814-07
Owner: Lars Lanke
Founded: 1967 (K)
Partnership (soc. nom collectif)
Capital: 40,000DH (K)
Turnover: 1,000,000-5,000,000DH (K)
Number of employees: 350-400 (K)
Hours of work (48-hour week): 0800-1230 and 1400-1730 (shut Sunday)

This rug-making establishment was housed in the old station of Salé-Bled. According to *Kompass,* the company has another workshop in Salé, route de la Plage, and a total of 80 looms.

In the workshop visited, there were 27 wooden looms in the high-roofed central hall and a further 12 in another equally high-ceilinged room. Both rooms were very draughty and were probably very cold in winter. When a train passed, the whole building shook. Cloth screens round the looms were possibly an attempt to reduce the draughts. The hours of work were well displayed in the workshop and there was a toilet and fire extinguisher.

About 95 women and children were at work, of whom about one-third looked under 12. Two *maalema* kept strict order.

The rugs were of a very high quality and it was not surprising to hear Mr Lanke say he was booked up to the end of 1978.

Production: unknown, mainly for export.

Above: Girls waiting to enter carpet factory.

Left: Makina factory, Fez, 1975.

Below: Girls embroidering in Meknès, 1975.

Bottom: Ensemble Artisanal, Tetuán, 1977.

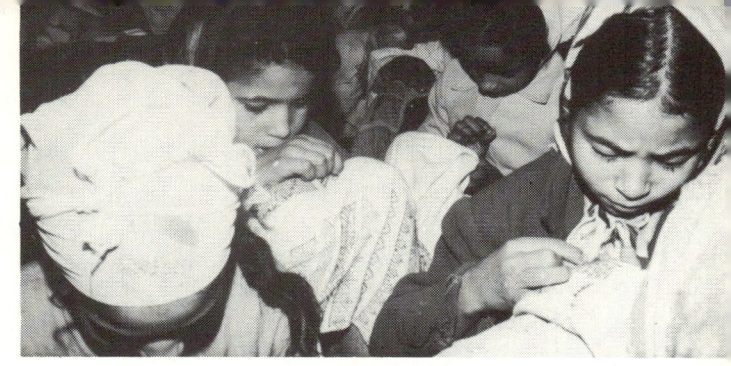

Left: Young girls embroidering, Meknès, 1975.

Below left: Ensemble Artisanal, Marrakesh, 1977.

Below right: Girl displaying embroidery.

Bottom: Nine girls working single loom in Coopérative Artisanale, Azrou, 1977. Girl on extreme left is very young.

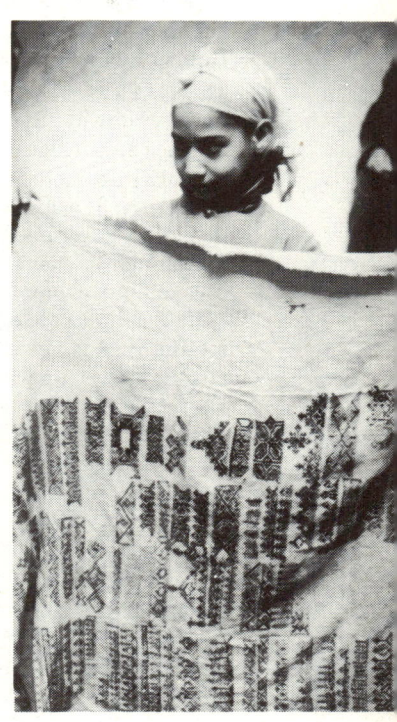

Styles: all kinds.
Prices: 200-250DH/sq.m. Moyen Atlas ("super-superior" quality).

REVISIT

SAFT (Société Africaine de Filature et Tissage), 9, avenue Al Maghreb el Arabi, Rabat. Telephone: 278-82.
Founded 1936.
Limited company (s.a.)
Capital: 6,975,000DH
Number of employees: 500 rug workers (1,000 workmen).
Hours of work (48-hour week): 0730-1200 and 1400-1730 (shut Sunday).

The SAFT is a very large textile company with branches in France, West Germany, Norway, Sweden, the United States and Australia, as well as in Rabat, Casablanca and Agadir.

Its activities include spinning and dyeing of wool, cloth-making and hand-knotted rugs. It supplies spun wool to many firms in Morocco. It is privately owned (*not* government-owned as was stated in previous report) and under European management.

The extensive premises in Rabat include rooms where carding, spinning and weaving machines are operated by male workers, as well as a large first floor area where the rug-makers are installed. A sick-room was noticed, as well as at least one large fire extinguisher, toilets and drinking water. The labour legislation was pinned up in the rug-making workshop.

The 150 looms, however, were very close together, with scarcely space to move between them. Even in April the room was stuffy and rather dusty. It was probably very hot in summer. Lighting was good.

Among the 500 workers were one or two small girls but the majority were girls in their teens or adult women. They sat about three or four to a loom. One woman or girl was responsible for each loom but the girls were engaged by the firm and not by a *maalema*.

There was a holiday of three weeks in the summer. The workers seemed happy and, apart from crowding and stuffiness, conditions were good. Part of the large workshop area was used for finishing rugs.

The whole premises gave a very good impression and the team was pleased to find that child labour was not used in this highly successful establishment.

Production: 4,000-5,000 sq.m./month, exported to France, West Germany, Europe generally and the USA and also for the home market.
Styles: all kinds.
Prices (retail): From 236DH/sq.m. (Fez) to 480DH/sq.m. (Rabat, 25/25).

Tangier

According to official figures, the production of rugs was the most important craft activity for the city and province of Tangier in 1975. Eleven cooperatives, employing between 4,000 and 5,000 workers, produced almost 160,000 square metres of rugs in the first six months of that year.

Rugs labelled "Moyen Atlas" were exclusively for export. The German Federal Republic was the most important client, followed by France, the Netherlands, Belgium and Canada. The turnover for these first six months reached 27,805,668DH. Tangier's production in 1976 was in fact only surpassed by Rabat.

Twelve commercial factories were visited as well as two government centres.

International Carpet Factory, 1, rue New York, Tangier. Telephone: 371-57.
Managing Director: Ben Yebdri Boumédienne (Algerian)
Number of employees: 600 (K)
Limited company (s.a.)
Capital: 60,800DH (K)
Hours of work: unknown (partially shut Saturday afternoon, shut Sunday)

Two companies under the same management occupied a large factory site beside three luxury hotels. Through the windows at least 100 looms could be seen.

A women waiting outside said that "very many" women and girls worked inside, including girls of 9 or 10. This was confirmed by a nearby bazaar owner. A few girls were seen finishing rugs in a large room. They were said not to leave at lunchtime but to eat on the premises.

No information on prices was available because, as a woman in the office explained, all work was done to order for West Germany, and they were fully booked well into the future. They made Moyen Atlas rugs, stamped in Tangier. Mr Boumédienne's brother was the owner of the factory seen in Sidi Moktar (see page 27).

Production: 5,000 sq.m./month (K)

MAFARTAP, 185, avenue Prince Heritier, Tangier. Telephone: 332-02
Director: Mr Mazari (Algerian)
Number of employees: "A great many", according to Mr Mazari.
Hours of work: until 1900 hours (shut Sunday).

It was not possible to visit the room in which girls could be heard at work making rugs. Through a series of windows looking out on to the street, the team could see four rows of looms fairly well apart in a room about 15 metres long. There were perhpas about 60 looms altogether. An employee said there were 300 but this seems unlikely.

Mr Mazari, speaking with reluctance, said he had three rug-making factories in Tangier and his order books were full to the end of October. He claimed to be the third most important producer of rugs for Morocco, from the point of view of quality.

Conveniently placed between two *bidonvilles,* Mr Mazari's factory had a ready source of labour. At lunchtime, a series of men and women could be seen going into the factory with baskets and coming out again shortly after without them.

An elderly man said that the employees worked a six-day week and had their lunch on the premises. He said he had two daughters working there and that conditions were very bad. One girl was paid 3.50DH a day, the other, a *maalema*, 5.50DH.

Between 1830 and 1900 hours, 86 girls were counted as they came out, 53 of whom were under 12. At 1900 hours the doors were shut.

Production: 7,000 sq.m./month (probably the three factories together, exported to West Germany and France).

Styles: specialising in Moyen Atlas.

Prices: 120-200DH according to quality and design.

Un-named workshop, 70, rue Allal ben Abdallah, Tangier

Owner: Cordelia (information from employee, but the workshop is probably Filature de Maghreb, SA. Telephone: 331-35, part of the International Carpet-Cordelia group.

Entry to this rather dilapidated establishment was absolutely refused. An old woman half-opened the gate and said that inquiries should be addressed to Mr Boumédienne at Cordelia. A large shed could just be seen. The place gave a very bad impression and private information from someone who had visited the factory was that conditions inside were very bad indeed.

Between 0650 and 0720 hours, 172 girls and children were seen arriving, 84 of whom were clearly under 12 — some as young as 6, 7 or 8. Many arrived with baskets. One was bare-footed. They were generally poorly dressed. No one arrived after 0720 hours.

Hamid Barghach and Oumnia Industriel, SA, 24, avenue de Lisbonne, Tangier. Telephone: 367-48 and 342-37

Owner: Hamid Barghach in association with an Algerian partner.

Mr Barghach was not available at the time of the visit and his nephew was unable to give any information. No looms or weavers were present at the premises, to which access was easy through an open gateway.

In a large open-fronted finishing hangar, two men and five girls were working. In another large well-lit room there were a few more girls. All these girls had been seen to arrive between 0650 and 0725 hrs.

This establishment was one of the few where the notices concerning the *Règlement de Travail* and *Accidents de Travail* were pinned up (in the office block).

Styles: Moyen Atlas.

103, Zankat Hauma Haj Said, Batouta (near Casa Barata quarter), Tangier.

A sheet of hardboard hid the interior of this workshop, which neighbours said was a rug-making concern. It was situated in a poor district on the out-skirts of the town. Inside what turned out to be a sort of garage were 15 looms.

Most of the girls were away at lunch, only six being on the premises at the time of the visit. One girl was under 12. The girls spoke readily and explained that the workshop belonged to Si Mohamed Meniali, whose office was "in front of the vegetable market". Mr Meniali was later identified with Oumnia Industriel, Mr Hamid Barghach's associate (see above).

The girls said the apprentices earned 1.75DH a day, the bigger girls a little more. One said that the money was better than going to school. They did not work on Sunday.

Anonymous workshop, a few hundred metres from the previous one (near Casa Barata quarter)
Owner: Hamid Barghach

A similar sheet of hardboard covered the front of this fairly large room. There were no means of telling that behind the hardboard was a workshop.

Inside were 20 looms and about 60 girls, many of them very young. The looms were close together and, as usual in these garage-type workshops, there were no windows.

A young man was in charge of the girls, who were all very excited by the unexpected and curious visit and eager to talk. They said they did not work on Sunday. The room was crowded although it was lunchtime. The girls said they worked for Mr Barghach.

Morocco Carpet, 104, route de Rabat, Km.2, Tangier (the old road).
Telephone: 389-83 (office).
Owner: Hamid Barghach
Number of employees: 200

In this large factory on the outskirts of Tangier a large room was packed with looms (43 counted but many more) and girls, often 10 or 12 to a loom. The great majority of the girls were well under 12.

Apart from over-crowding, conditions were good. The room was well-lit and well-ventilated. There was a toilet. An employee responsible for the designs and the running of the factory said there were 200 workers and no *maalema*.

Styles: Moyen Atlas.

SONAFITI, SA (Société Nationale de Filature et Tissage), 12, rue Legazpi, Tangier (beside Dispensaire Anti-Tuberculose, below Kasba, near cemetary). Telephone: 211-93.
Director: Mr Bencherida.

The address visited was the head office and no rug makers were seen. Mr Bencherida was not available to give information on prices but a man in the office said the company had four factories in Tangier. They also produced textiles.

No information was available on staff or hours of work, but outside information was that they employed women and young girls.

Production: 2,000 sq.m./month.
Styles: Moyen Atlas.

Tanger Carpet, 24, rue Quevado, appartement 11, Tangier. Telephone: 214-49
Directors: Mr Khamal and Mr Lahlou

The address visited was merely the office and no rug-workers were present. One of the directors said they had four factories in Tangier and planned to open two more in Rabat. Their wool was imported spun and dyed from France. If the client requested, Moroccan wool was used and prices were then lower.

Production: 3,500 sq.m./month.
Prices: Plain, plyed wool, 150DH/sq.m., simple pattern 20-40% more, long pile and Rabat, 300-400DH/sq.m.

Factory, Km.3, route de Rabat, Tangier (the old road)

This new factory turned out to belong to Tanger Carpet. A director on the premises said they were in full expansion. A total of 3,500-4,000 square metres were produced monthly in this factory and they hoped to reach 5,000 sq.m./month.

No information was available on staff but it was said that young girls worked for this company.

Etablissement Zitan – Manufacture Rachidi, 128 Amerigo Vespucci, Docks Monopole, Tangier.
Owner: Mohamed Ahmed Zitan
Director: Mohamed Taieb Amrani
Number of employees: 2,500 (total staff in all factories).

This vast family concern covered a variety of textile operations in several towns: spinning, dyeing and weaving in Chechaouen, Tetuán, Ouezzane, Meknès, Fez and Tangier (see pages 21, 28, 31 and 44). In Tangier alone, Manufacture Rachidi had 15 carpet factories, according to the director (Mr Zitan's son-in-law).

The director was extremely helpful and pleased to display his rugs and talk about his business. According to the Tangier Chamber of Commerce, the firm was the third most important in Tangier. In March 1977 alone, he said, he had produced 12,000 square metres, and that in 1976 his company had produced 90,000 square metres. He hoped to exceed 100,000 square metres for 1977. A second workshop with 100 looms was shortly to be opened on the site visited.

The present premises were extensive, with large finishing, packing and storage hangars, as well as the workshop. Some 30 girls were busy finishing a number of rugs.

In the workshop about 150 girls were working about 30-40 looms, with an average of five girls per loom. At least 58 girls under 12 were noted and many appeared to be 9 or 10 at the most. The looms were very close together but lighting and air were good.

The director had nothing to do with engaging the girls. This was the responsibility of the *maalema* in charge of each loom. He did not know exactly how many workers were in the factory, but his total staff amounted to 2,500 workers.

Manufacture Rachidi imported its wool, at a rate of 130,000-150,000 kilos per month. The firm kept some for itself after spinning, and the rest was sold. All the finished rugs, wherever made, were stamped in Tangier.

When asked if he had any labour problems, the director replied: "Well, yes, a bit, and it is likely to get worse. There are more and more schools and with increasing education it will be difficult to get the little girls". As for adult female labour, he said that women had difficulty leaving their houses.

Production: 11,000-12,000 sq.m./month (all factories), exported to Europe.
Styles: all kinds.
Prices: plain — 127DH/sq.m., simple design — 130DH/sq.m., simple design but more heavily packed (15/15) — 165DH/sq.m., round rugs — 150DH/sq.m., modern, in relief — 150DH/sq.m.

Abdallah Boughaba, 119 and 128, rue de Fés, Tangier. Telephone: 349-23
Owner: Abdallah Boughaba
Hours of work: 6 days a week (shut Sunday)

The Boughaba premises are on each side of the road. Abdallah Boughaba's brother said that they had 20 looms with about four girls per loom. He did not give the total figure of workers.

In the workshop visited there were four looms and 14 girls and one *maalema* were counted. Ten of the girls were very young. They were still at work at 1815 hours on Saturday.

The unvisited workshop opposite was said by other informants who had seen it to be very cramped. Conditions in the room visited were average.

Production: 100 sq.m./month (Rabat rugs take a long time to make), for local market, but there had been a recent sale to Sweden.
Style: specialising in Rabat.
Prices: Moyen Atlas, simple design — 150DH/sq.m., round or modern — 250DH/sq.m., Rabat — 220-500DH/sq.m. according to wool.

Tetuań

The number of rugs officially stamped in Tetuán is very small — under 200 in 1975. However, it seemed that many rug factories in Tatuán were owned by Tangier firms and the rugs were inspected and stamped not in Tetuán but in Tangier.

Information was obtained on three industrialized rug factories, although entry was forbidden. One state craft enterprise was visited.

Fabrica Bab Tout (marked "Maderas-Cristales", but now a rug factory), Tetuán.
Manager: Mr Benchekroun
Owner: International Carpet Factory, Tangier
Number of employees: 400-500 (600 according to Direction de l'Artisanat)
Hours of work (60-hour week): 0700 to 1230 and 1400 to 1830 (shut Sunday).
Information from Direction de l'Artisanat, Tetuán.

Entry to this factory was refused. Some women waiting in the doorway said that "many" women and children worked there. Later, a male employee came out and volunteered the information that 400-500 women and girls were employed and that the owner was an Algerian living in Tangier, where he had 10 other factories (see page 39).

The employee said the workers were paid 2.50-3.00DH a day and the *maalema* a certain sum per square metre. He said the rugs were of a high quality and if there was the slightest defect they were rejected.

A total of 353 women and children were counted as they came out for lunch between 1230 and 1255 hours. A total of 86 were adult women (two of them elderly), 89 were girls of 12 to 16 or 17, and 178 were very young children all under 12.

Production: 3-4,000 sq.m;/month for export to Europe (information from Direction de l'Artisanat).

Anonymous factory behind Prison Civile, Quartier Rigulalez, Tetuán
Owner: Manufacture Rachidi, Tangier

The usual large metal sliding door was the only hint that this was a carpet factory — apart from the chanting of the children would could be heard from outside. The door being slightly open, it was possible to see a large room with some 30 looms packed closely together. There were probably about 60 on the premises.

A great many girls could be seen, the majority of them very young (under 12). Activity was intense, lighting and air were moderately good. Two male employees, angry at the interruption, immediately came forward and said that visitors were not allowed.

They said, however, that the factory was new, that it belonged to Manufacture Rachidi of Tangier (see page 42) and employed some 240 girls. The rugs were officially stamped in Tangier.

Anonymous factory, rue Chakib Arssalane (ex-Centre Culturel Francais), Tetuán
Owner: Manufacture Rachidi

The Direction de l'Artisanat said this new factory had only just been opened and was a branch of a Tangier firm. There was nothing on the door to indicate it was a factory and entry was firmly refused.

It was possible, however, to see a large room in which 12 girls were busy finishing the rugs. There were no looms, and all the girls were over 12. An employee said it belonged to Manufacture Rachidi, which had another one up near the prison (see above).

5. State-Run Establishments

Government-sponsored handicraft cooperatives exist in many Moroccan towns. They are generally housed in modern buildings and tourists are encouraged to visit them. They are principally sales outlets but craftsmen can usually be watched at work on the premises.

It was originally hoped that these cooperatives would help the craftworker to compete in an increasingly industrialized world. It seems *(Lamalif,* No.86, February/March 1977) that they have not been entirely successful: of 113 cooperatives existing in 1972, only 72 are still active and of these only 45 are actually engaged in production.

Their activities are the responsibility of the Secrétariat d'Etat chargé de l'Artisanat et de l'Entre'aide Nationale, and the women and children employed in the rug-making and embroidery cooperatives are not "salaried workers in the sense of the current Moroccan labour legislation" (letter of 14 January 1976 from the Moroccan embassy in London to the Anti-Slavery Society).

It should be borne in mind that these cooperatives are not groups of producers working together to share costs and benefits: they are simply undertakings run by the state on commercial lines, with the workers receiving some sort of remuneration for their work. Each cooperative is a semi-autonomous body with its own hours of work, system of recruitement, remuneration and prices.

It was not surprising that conditions varied, from the strict *maalema* system at Azrou, with the children engaged and paid by her, to the more relaxed atmosphere at Chichaoua or Tetuán. Working conditions were generally better and hours of work shorter than in the average factory.

It was often difficult to distinguish schools of apprenticeship from a new craft centre with apprentices. In many cases the former had been merged with the latter. They are therefore all included in this chapter.

REVISIT

Coopérative Artisanale, Azrou
Hours of work (39-hour week): 0830 to 1200 and 1430 to 1730 (shut Friday)

At the time of the visit, the cooperative was still shut for lunch. A number of children were waiting on the other side of the road — "nothing to with the cooperative," said the doorman. When spoken to, these girls — who were, of course, workers — were ready and pleased to talk until opening time. Their gaiety and frankness was in striking contrast with the discipline encountered once they were back at work.

All the children spoken to — about 30 or 40 — were emphatic that they earned no money. They were apprentices. They would begin earning later: they were not sure when, perhaps in a year or a year and a half. They were not sure how much they would be paid: it depended on how good they were.

Only one said she had been to school. The rest said they had had no schooling and none seemed to have been to the Koranic school. It seems that three years ago classes were given in the cooperative but that this has been stopped. Several girls said they enjoyed their work.

Inside, some 140 girls were actively at work on the looms. They were constantly on the move and there was quite a number of them engaged in other operations, such as wool-sorting, fetching skeins and so on. The figure of 300 noted in the previous report was not counted on the day of the visit.

One girl spoken to outside said she was 10, another was probably about 7, having not yet replaced her two front milk teeth. The great majority of the girls seen were under 12, though there were some older girls of about 15 or 16. Those spoken to lived in Azrou itself.

Supervising the children were older women. When asked how many children worked a loom, one replied sharply "ask the manager".

Twenty-five looms were noted, with a maximum of eight to 10 children per loom, sometimes packed very tightly together on their benches. Conversation with the children was no longer possible once they got back to work, for the *maalema,* who had disapprovingly noted the earlier conversation outside, discouraged further contact.

The manager, a well-dressed middle-aged Moroccan with a secretary, was not able to give production figures. He was very much on the defensive and replied at once that "the girls were not forced to work, it was a cooperative, with one family to each loom".

"One family" should be taken to mean that the *maalema* in charge of each loom recruits the children she knows, not necessarily from her own family but at least among her acquaintances. The manager said they were planning to separate the handicrafts for sale from the workshop. Visitors would then no longer be able to see the employees at work.

It was difficult to ascertain the salaries of the *maalema* and the time taken to weave a square metre. One girl volunteered that the *maalema* received 25DH per square metre. This figure is lower than the average noted by the 1975 team but was representative of other factories visited.

A square metre represents at least a day's work, depending on the complexity of the design and the number of workers involved. To judge from the sales prices, this would mean at least 200DH remaining after the *maalema* had been paid, and it seems very unlikely that all of this sum could have gone on raw materials and overheads.

The premises were pleasant, well-lit by natural light, clean and airy, constructed around an open-air courtyard with a fountain. There were four toilets, allotted separately for men and for women. Drinking water was available.

There was no summer holiday and its seems doubtful that there was any medical control. There was no difficulty in taking photographs (see photographs).

Prices: (retail) 230-290DH/sq.m.

Centre d'Apprentissage de Broderie et Tapis, rue d'Anfa, ancienne Medina, Casablanca

Hours of work: all week but shut Saturday afternoon and Sunday.

This centre is run by the Direction de l'Artisanat. Some 30-40 girls were sitting idle behind their looms at the time of the visit, for they had run out of wool. The 10 looms were well separated, the room well-aired and light, looking on to a good-sized courtyard. About 40 girls were busy on embroidery in an adjoining room. None of the girls seen in either group was under 12.

The rug-makers said they were paid 120DH a month. They were apparently apprentices. They seemed happy with their lot and the embroiderers were keen to show off their work. A few of these latter spoke a word or two of French.

Agence Artisanale, Entre'aide Nationale, Chechaouen

Hours of work (37½-hour week): 0800-1200 and 1430-1800 (shut Saturday and Sunday).

Seventeen girls and one young *maalema* were at work. Two girls were aged about 9 or 10. There were 12 looms but many were not in use. An average of four girls worked at one loom. In 15 days, two of them could make two square metres of a slightly complicated rug.

It was said that they had all been to school and were "well paid". There was no discipline, the girls were in high spirits and eager to talk. The room was well-lit and airy.

Société Coopérative Artisanale — Tapis Chichaoua, Chichaoua (Province Marrakech)

Hours of work (40-hour week): 0800-1200 and 1400-1800 (shut Friday and Sunday).

A few rugs made by local women were on display in this government centre. The man in charge said that the present building — a simple Moroccan country house of mud-bricks — was to be pulled down and replaced by a new building, with accommodation for the weavers and their families.

Two girls, about 13 and 14 (probably family), were working on a loom in one of the rooms. Friday and Sunday were officially non-working days, but if there was an order to fulfil they would work these days. Only locally-made rugs were sold there, and the workers were paid for their work by the state.

Prices: approximately 137DH/sq.m.

Ensemble Artisanal (near Holiday Inn Hotel), Fez
Hours of work (44-hour week): 0800-1200 and 1400-1800 (shut Saturday afternoon and Sunday).

This was a newly-built craft centre, with a display room and several workshops. In one room 20 teenage girls were doing embroidery. In another 30 apprentice embroiderers were at work. The weaving workshop housed 11 looms fairly close together.

It was said that there was one *maalema* in charge of each loom (five were seen), and she was responsible for recruiting and paying her workers. She herself was paid for the work done. The girls sat six or seven to a loom and at least half of the 50 or 60 girls counted were well under 12.

The atmosphere somewhat resembled that at Azrou, with many young girls and a number of severe *maalema*. The premises were light and airy and looked on to a courtyard/garden.

Société Coopérative Artisanale de Brodeuses de Fes — Centre d'Apprentissage de Broderie (Direction de l'Artisanat), Fes (besides Palais Dar el Beida)
Hours of work (39-hour week): 0830-1200 and 1500-1800 (shut Sunday).

Only skilled workers worked here: the apprentices were lodged elsewhere (probably in the Ensemble Artisanal). There were 30 qualified girls in their teens in this aristocratic Fez house, with balconies and airy, well-lit rooms. There was a toilet.

It was said that apprentices could start as young as 7 or 8, and after a certain length of time they took an exam to become recognized as qualified workers. No information was available on the pay received by a qualified worker.

Ensemble Artisanal, avenue Mohamed V, Kenitra
Hours of work (48-hour week): 0800-1200 and 1400-1800 (shut Sunday).

This was a modern building opened only two years ago. A number of large well-lit rooms looked on to a central courtyard with flowers and a fountain.

In one room some 80 embroiders were at work. In another 60 girls (said to be the total) were at work on 17 looms.

Conditions of work were excellent. No young girls were seen in either group and the one *maalema* in charge of the weaving — a middle-aged Arabic-speaking Moroccan — explained that no child under 12 was engaged and that all had had primary schooling.

The apprentices were paid 2DH a day. At the end of two years they were given a diploma and became qualified workers. No information on wages at this stage was available but several girls said the work was "good". A number spoke a little French and were pleased to talk.

Production: 50 sq.m./month (five rugs), said to be high quality work.
Price: 300DH/sq.m.

Coopérative Artisanale, avenue Mohamed V, Khemisset

Hours of work (41-hour week): 0830-1200 and 1400-1800 (shut Friday).

Woodworking and rug-making were the specialities of this cooperative. There were 22 looms in a large well-lit room and 50 girls were counted. It was possible to move about freely, talk to the girls and take photographs. The atmosphere was pleasant and far removed from that at Azrou.

One girl said there were generally 100 workers. The majority were aged 14-16. though there were a number of small girls, some said to be as young as 8. One or two women supervised proceedings but the girls were not recruited by the *maalema*.

Several girls said that the apprentices did at least a year's training, during which time they were paid 25DH a month. The qualified girls got 200DH a month. (See photographs).

Prices (retail): Rabat 455DH/sq.m., Zemmour 300-410DH/sq.m., modern 355DH/sq.m.

Ensemble Artisanal, avenue Mohamed V, Marrakesh

Hours of work (42-hour week): 0800-1200 and 1500-1800 (shut Sunday)
Display centre open 0830-1200 and 1430-1900.

This modern and attractively laid-out Moroccan-style centre, with stucco work, glazed tiling and fountains, was inaugurated on 8th March 1977 and has been functioning since October 1975. A wide variety of craft goods are on sale on the premises, but the workshops for the craftworkers are housed apart. Many tourists were present, buying, watching the weavers at work or taking photographs.

The weaving workshop was large, well-ventilated, well-lit with large windows looking on to an open courtyard.

Some 20 girls were at work but not all 14 looms were in use. Generally two or four girls worked a loom, occasionally six. At least six or seven of the girls were no more than 10 years old, others were about 14 or 15 and one could have been as old as 20. No adult women were present, nor could any *maalema* be seen. In a large adjoining room a girl was clipping a carpet.

The children spoke with great freedom and spontaneity, inviting visitors to sit down and work with them. Most who were spoken to said they earned nothing and asked for a *dirham*. Two said they occasionally got some cooking oil. Two others, aged about 14, said they earned 2.50DH a day and a third, smaller, gave the rather high figure of 5DH a day. They said it took two days to do a square metre of simple rug.

All except one were from Marrakesh. The exception was a small girl from Ouarzazate who had relatives in Marrakesh. All said they enjoyed the work and they certainly seemed quite carefree. They had one month's unpaid holiday in the summer. There appeared to be no discipline.

Prices (retail): variable, but two carpets looked at came to about 180DH/sq.m.

Ensemble Artisanal, Meknès

Number of employees: 40 cooperative members (rug-making), 80-100 apprentices (rug-making)

Hours of work (41-hour week): 0830-1200 and 1400-1800 (shut Saturday afternoon and Sunday).

This new building, opened only a few months ago, contains not only a rug-making cooperative but also incorporates several schools of apprenticeship.

The young manager was extremely friendly and helpful. He explained that there were 40 women rug-makers, members of the cooperative. In addition there were 80-100 apprentices (not yet cooperative members) who did two years' unpaid apprenticeship.

There were 22 looms, with an average of two cooperative members and five apprentices per loom. Their wool was Moroccan. The looms were well separated. The room was large, well-lit, well aired and looked out on to an open courtyard.

The manager said that the cooperative members were paid for each square metre produced, according to the net profits of the cooperative. He did not say how much this sum generally was. He also said that all the girls were over 12 and had been to school, though it was noted that several small girls of 10 and 11 were at work.

The atmosphere was relaxed and friendly and the manager said he was on excellent terms with the workers. As an indication of salaries, it is interesting to note that he himself was paid only 600DH a month and had to supplement this by giving music lessons.

Styles: all kinds, to order.

Production: 100 sq.m./month but order just received from West Germany for 1,500 sq.m. to be delivered in 1977.

Prices: Moyen Atlas — 170-180DH/sq.m., Rabat (30/30) — 350DH/sq.m., (40/30) — 400-450DH/sq.m., Modern (20/20) — 280DH/sq.m.

Embroidery workshop

In another room were 20 apprentice embroiderers, all over 12. They sat on the floor on rugs against the wall of a well-lit room. There was one qualified girl in charge.

The apprentices qualified for admission by means of an exam, then did two years of apprenticeship before taking another exam to become qualified workers. During their apprenticeship they were paid 2DH a day, amounting to some 40 or 50DH a month, according to the number of days actually worked.

Coopérative de Tisseuses — Centre de Formation et de l'Emploi pour le Mers, avenue el Mers, Meknès

Hours of work (38½-hour week): 0830-1200 and 1400-1800 (shut Saturday afternoon and Sunday).

This state cooperative, under the auspices of Entre'aide Nationale, housed girls working knitting machines and doing various other activities, as well as the rug-making cooperative.

There were said to be 24 female instructors and some 600-700 girls learning various crafts in this clean, well-lit building. The embroiderers were all neatly dressed in white overalls but it was not possible to visit the weaving workshop since the directress was absent.

A member of the staff said there were two groups of weavers, 20 in each group, one group in the morning and one in the afternoon. In each group there were *maalema* and apprentices, but it was not possible to find out the age of the apprentices, other than that they were "young".

Styles: Moyen Atlas, Rabat, modern (all made to order).

Direction de l'Artisanat, Agence de l'Artisanat, Ouezzane

Some 30 weavers were working in this government establishment. About 20 other girls, all well over 12, were working on embroidery in one of the rooms. The weavers were in their teens and had finished primary schooling. All were apprentices, earning 2DH a day. After two years' training, they would become qualified workers.

There were 14 looms and working conditions were very good, with plenty of air and light.

REVISIT

Coopérative des Tisseuses de tapis des Oudayas, Kasba des Oudayas, Rabat
Hours of work (46½-hour week): 0800-1200 and 1400-1830 (shut Saturday afternoon and Sunday).

This cooperative, deep in the Kasba (old quarter), was housed in three darkish rooms — one for display and two for rug-making. There was a small courtyard. One working room was lit by neon lighting, the other by daylight. There were 24 looms, well separated from each other, about an equal number in each room. The rooms were low roofed and not very large.

A total of 43 weavers were at work, including one or two women. Seven girls were probably under 12, while the rest were in their teens.

One girl questioned said that she was a qualified worker but would not say how much she earned except that it was a weekly wage. A male employee said that some girls were apprentices and were paid "pocket-money". The others were paid 25DH a square metre. One girl said it took 10 days to make a square metre.

Several girls spoke a little French and had been to school. Outside information was that the girls were paid 3DH a day. There was no feeling of constraint or discipline and the girls talked freely to the tourists who came in.

Prices (retail): Rabat 400DH/sq.m.

Centre d'Apprentissage, Kasba, Tangier
Hours of work (45-hour week): 0800-1200 and 1430-1800 (shut Sunday).

The weaving section had recently been transferred to the Grottes d'Hercule,

18 kilometres outside Tangier. In the Kasba, eight girls were doing embroidery (all over 12). Conditions of work were good. It was run by the Direction de l'Artisanat.

Ensemble Artisanal, Grottes d'Hercule, Tangier

This modern centre, as yet unfinished, housed six looms and a total of 46 girls (the Direction de l'Artisanat at the Kasba said there were 30). Ten of the 20-odd girls seen were almost certainly under 12. They came from the surrounding villages. Some went home for lunch, others ate on the premises.

Conditions were very good, with a central open courtyard, running water and well-lit, airy and uncrowded rooms. All the girls were apprentices, but they were apparently paid a small daily wage. There was no summer holiday.

Four modern rugs were on display that were to be copied by the apprentices. They were said to learn quickly. The girls were gay and undisciplined and the atmosphere agreeable. There was keen competition to be photographed.

Centre d'Education et Travail, Taroudant
Hours of work (42-hour week): 0830-1200 and 1430-1800 (shut Sunday).

At the time of the visit this school of apprenticeship, run by Entre'aide Nationale, was shut for the spring holiday. Information was supplied by a helpful French-speaking Moroccan woman in the office of this building, which used to be the Orphelinat Lalla Aicha.

She said that some 900 children received various kinds of training, including training in embroidery and rug-making. School holidays were observed, with the exception of the summer, when there was only one month's holiday.

Older girls did two years' apprenticeship in rug-making, then sat an exam and could become in their turn instructresses in various government centres, or take up whatever employment they wanted.

Small girls could become apprentices from 8 years of age onwards, but in this case they did more than two years' apprenticeship. All apprentices were unpaid. All saleable work was the property of the state.

Government cooperative, Tazenakht

This establishment was not visited, but was said by the Chambre d'Artisanat of Marrakesh to have 60 looms and to employ many women and children to do work on the premises.

Ensemble Artisanal, Tetuán
Hours of work (46½-hour week): 0800-1200 and 1430-1900 (shut Saturday
    afternoon and Sunday).

This vast modern building includes a large room displaying a variety of craftwork, together with rooms where weavers or leatherworkers can be seen working. It was opened four years ago.

Two spacious, well-lit, sunny rooms housed a number of looms, many not in use. There was an average of four girls per loom, the looms being arranged around the wall so as to leave a large open space in the middle of the room.

Twenty-three girls and adult women were at work. A baby was sleeping on the bench beside his mother. At least one girl was under 12. The girls said they earned 3DH a day. There was one month's holiday in the summer (unpaid).

Working conditions were very good. There was no difficulty either in talking to the girls or in photographing them. There was no overseer. Many wanted copies of the photographs.

No information was avilable on production and prices as the display centre was closed.

6. Moroccan Labour Legislation

The Moroccan government lodges its labour legislation with the International Labour Office in Geneva, along with other signatories to the ILO conventions. The legislation currently in force, according to ILO records, is the decree of 2 July 1947 *(Bulletin Officiel,* 17 October 1947, No.1825, p.1028). Several additions and amendments have been made to this decree but it nevertheless remains the basic labour legislation in Morocco today.

Among the items of relevance to the present report are the following:

1. The Labour Inspectorate is responsible for the application of social legislation. It covers industrial and commercial enterprises and their annexes as well as craft establishment and cooperatives (Dahir of 2 July 1947).
2. Children under the age of 12 may not be engaged or employed as workers, employees or apprentices (Dahir of 2 July 1947).
3. All paid workers, including unqualified labourers, must be employed through state employment offices (Dahir of 7 May 1940).
4. The Model Statute must be publicly displayed (Dahir of 23 October 1948).
5. The minimum salary for industrial and commercial workers is fixed at 1.40DH per hour (application No.2.77.52 of 28 December 1976). Agricultural workers to get a minimum of 7.25DH a day. Children of 12-15 to get 50% less, and from 15-18 30% less.
6. The minimum salary is also fixed for "certain" work done at home, in particular in the clothing industry (Dahir of 20 December 1939).
7. A long-service bonus must be added to the salaries of all workers, rising progressively after two years of service (Dahirs of 24 January 1953 and 30 December 1972).
8. A sub-contractor supplying labour to a principal contractor must not make a profit of more than 10% in so doing (Dahir of 24 January 1953).
9. Working hours for men and women, whatever their age, shall not exceed eight hours a day or 48 hours a week (Dahir of 18 June 1936).
10. Official holidays are paid at the same rate as the daily wage the worker would have received, or a proportional sum in the case of piece-work (Dahir of 21 July 1947).

11. Wage earners have the right to a paid holiday of 1½ days for every month of work. Workers and apprentices under 18 have the right to two days paid holiday for every month worked (Dahir of 9 January 1946).

12. People working at home have the right to an annual paid holiday (Arrêté of 9 March 1946).

13. General rules on hygiene, air space, heating, dust, availability of drinking water and prohibition on eating meals in the workshops are laid down in the Dahir of 2 July 1947.

14. Establishments employing more than 50 workers must arrange for a regular medical service (Dahir of 8 July 1957).

In connection with these points, the following facts emerge from visits to more than 60 premises:

— Work inspectors very seldom call and generally expect to be paid for their silence.*

— The employment of children under 12, both as workers and apprentices, was commonplace.

— Many employers had nothing to do with the recruitment of the girls working the looms. They were certainly not engaged through the local state employment office. The practice of letting a *maalema* recruit children seems to come close to the forbidden "sub-contracting" system.

— The minimum salary was generally not paid. Fixed at 0.70DH an hour for children from 12-15, it would mean a daily wage of 5.60-6.30DH. The increase for long service was certainly not paid.

— In very few establishments was any kind of legislation noticeably displayed.

— It seems unlikely that either minimum salaries or paid holidays were applied to home workers.

— The working week frequently exceeded the legal figure for *adults:* 14 of the 29 premises for which information was obtained worked a week of more than 50 hours and two of them worked as much as 72 hours.

— Official holidays may possibly have been paid (no information), but cases of a paid annual holiday were extremely rare.

— In general, the establishments visited had some sort of toilet, but the eating of meals in the workshop was common. (A stove and stewpot were even in use behind the bench of a group of girls working a loom in one Casablanca workshop). Lighting, heating and air space were often inadequate.

— In only one establishment was a regular medical visit arranged by the owner.

*It was difficult to bring up the question of work inspectors when visiting the factories. The few cases where it was possible to do so and conversations with private contacts indicated there has been no noticeable increase in the inspectors' activity since presentation of the Anti-Slavery Society's first report in March 1975 to the Moroccan government.

7. Conclusions and Recommendations

The use of child labour in carpet factories in Morocco violates basic human rights and domestic legislation. Yet, the employment of children is expanding rapidly with the growth of the industry.

Moroccan labour legislation represents on paper a genuine desire to safeguard the welfare of the worker. The Moroccan government, in its reply to the Anti-Slavery Society dated 14 January 1976, emphasized that workers in craft enterprises are fully covered by this legislation. It therefore remains a matter of some surprise and concern that, as shown in the preceding chapter, such a wide gap should exist between the theory and the practice.

The Moroccan government may perhaps consider it desirable to enact legislation which, though as yet unenforceable, should help to raise standards eventually by educating public opinion. Nevertheless, it is surely undesirable to present to the outside world a series of laws that are largely disregarded.

A principal cause of and excuse for violation of labour regulations is the employment by factory owners of *maalema* or *maitresses:* women who, having graduated from the looms, are made responsible for the recruitment, training, supervision, administration, discipline, and, if they so wish, dismissal of the girl-workers. Some *maalema* are as young as 17.

The system was formerly standard practice when rugs were made in private houses and when treatment of the workers varied from benevolent paternalism to slavery. Now transferred to the factories, though labour may be lawfully recruited only through a state employment office, the system provides a means whereby factory owners can, if the law is not enforced, avoid all contact with their workers.

Though government-owned factories generally conform with the law in regard to recruitment and in most respects set a high standard, the *maalema* survives in a few state factories as well as in most of those in the private sector.

The eradication of this system is considered to be a necessary — and practicable — first step towards reform of working conditions. Its elimination would mean that factory owners would no longer excuse themselves from direct responsibility for their workers.

The Anti-Slavery Society recognizes that a remedy for the exploitation of children in carpet manufacturing cannot be found in isolation from broader social and economic issues. However, the employment of children aged from 8, or even less, to 12 years, for as long, in some instances as 72 hours per week, often for no pay at all, should not be tolerated in a country with Morocco's aspirations and standing. The very good conditions in government factories generally gives ground for hope that the situation in private factories will be improved.

The Anti-Slavery Society urges:

a. that the Moroccan government extend firm control over conditions in private carpet factories to bring these conditions at least up to the standard now existing in government factories.

b. that the Labour Inspectorate be given the means to carry out effectively its task in carpet factories and other craft establishments, and in particular to enforce existing legislation on the minimum age for employment (Dahir of 2 July 1947), on hours of work (Dahir of 18 June 1936) and on hygiene and safety (Dahir of 2 July 1947).

Responsibility for enforcement of labour legislation belongs to the Government of Morocco alone. Nevertheless the Anti-Slavery Society urges that the government consider seeking the assistance of the International Labour Organization in studying how working conditions in the carpet and other craft industries can be brought into line with Morocco's domestic legislation and with the international standards, of which Morocco has informally expressed its acceptance.

Appendix A. Moroccan Education

The Moroccan population is a young one: 56% of its 17 million inhabitants are under 20 (1975 figures). Children of primary school age and younger are represented as follows:

0-4	3,072,000	(boys: 1,554,000;	girls: 1,518,000)
5-9	2,625,000	(boys: 1,322,000;	girls: 1,303,000)
10-14	2,196,000	(boys: 1,099,000;	girls: 1,097,000)

Despite efforts made by the government, it has proved impossible to provide education for all these children. This is particularly so in the rural areas. Figures for 1974-75 show that some 1,400,000 children attended primary school (state and private). At least 2 million children of primary age did not attend school. School attendance is not for the moment obligatory and it is difficult to see it becoming so in the near future with an ever-increasing population.

Pre-primary education (up to the age of 7) is provided by the traditional Koranic schools. Two years' attendance at the Koranic school is essential if a child is to continue in a state school.

Primary education officially starts at the age of 7. By the age of 12, a child must either leave school or qualify to continue with secondary education. Only a very small proportion of children go on to secondary education. Primary school is generally on a rota system and half-time: a teacher may have 100 pupils, only half of whom are present in the school at any given moment. In the third year mathematics and French are taught in French, all other subjects continuing in Arabic.

It is ironic that the age limits are more strictly observed at school than they are in the factory. It is far more difficult to stay on at school after the official age than it is to be taken on at the factory under the legal age.

Girls are particularly disfavoured as regards schooling. According to official figures, one girl out of four attends primary school compared with one boy out of two. The 1.5 million girls who do not attend primary school offer a cheap and ready labour force.

It is unfortunate too that this situation, far from getting better in the near future, it likely to deteriorate. Even with the best will in the world, the present yearly increase in population far exceeds the country's educational possibilities.

Source: Secrétariat d'Etat auprès du Premier Ministre chargé du Plan et du Développement Régional, 1975.

Appendix B. Correspondence

From: The Secretary of the Anti-Slavery Society
To: The Moroccan Ambassador in London

UN#29   8 May 1975

Your Excellency,

      In its capacity as a non-governmental organization in consultative relationship with the United Nations Economic and Social Council this Society has been asked by the Director of the United Nations Division of Human Rights to contribute any information it may possess on contemporary infractions of (inter alia) the UN Supplementary Convention on the Abolition of Slavery, the Slave Trade and Institutions and Practices Similar to Slavery, 1956.
      One of the practices which (though not, of course, amounting to slavery) parties to this Convention undertake to forbid may be described for the sake of brevity as the exploitation of children.

      In this connection this Society has recently made a study of conditions in some of the privately-owned carpet factories in Morocco. I enclose our report and would respectfully ask Your Excellency to bring it to the notice of Your Government and to say that my Committee will be grateful for Your Government's comments which we would wish to send to the United Nations.

               I have the honour to be

               Your Excellency's humble servant

                                   SECRETARY

His Excellency The Moroccan Ambassador

Londres, le 14 Janvier, 1976.

L'Ambassadeur de Sa Majesté le Roi,
à Londres,

ECO/ca.   000077

A

Monsieur le Secrétaire Général de
L'Association contre l'esclavage
et pour la Protection des droits
de l'homme.
60 Weymouth Street,
LONDON, W1N 4DX.

Your Ref: UN/29.

Objet: Conditions de travail dans les manufactures
de tapis au Maroc.

Référence: Votre correspondance N° UN/29 du 30 octobre 1975.
Ma lettre ECO/ca du 15 octobre 1975.

Suite à nos correspondance citées en référence, j'ai l'honneur de vous communiquer ci-après les
éléments d'appréciation formulés par le Ministère
Marocain du travail et des affaires sociales et relatifs
à votre requête citée en objet.

Par ailleur, veuillez bien trouver, ci-joint,
pour information, et émanant du Ministère précité un
bref aperçu sur la genède du problème de l'assujettisse-
ment du secteur artisanal à la législation du travail
et en particulier aux dispositions relatives à la sécurité et à l'hygiène professionnelle et locale.

.../...

Abdellatif NACIF
Premier Secrétaire.

I. CONDITIONS DE TRAVAIL DANS LES MANUFACTURES DE TAPIS AU MAROC.

1) Afin d'examiner sur place les conditions de travail des enfants dans les manufactures de tapis, les représentants de l'Association ci-dessus mentionnée ont été amenés à visiter des établissements de trois catégories différentes: des fabriques de tapis, des coopératives artisanales et des école d'apprentissage.

Dans ces deux dernières catégories d'établissements, les femmes et les enfants ne sont pas salariés au sens de la législation du travail en vigueur et l'activité s'exerce sous la tutelle du Secrétariat d'Etat Chargé de l'Artisanat et de l'Entraide Nationale.

En ce qui concerne les fabriques de tapis exploitées soit par de petits artisans, soit par des employeurs occupant un grand nombre d'ouvrières, il s'agit d'établissement assujettis à la législation du travail, notamment en matière de conditions d'emploi des enfants.

2) A cet égard, il convient de souligner, ainsi d'ailleurs que le relève le rapport, que le dahir du 13 chaabane 1366 (2 juillet 1974) portant réglementation du travail a fixé à douze ans l'âge d'admission des enfants au travail ou à l'apprentissage.

De plus et compte tenu du fait que dans le secteur artisanal, certaines pratiques dûes aux conditions particulières de travail mais non conformes à la législation avaient été constatées, le Ministre du travail et des affaires sociales a cru nécessaire dès le 11 octobre 1956 de rappeler par circulaire aux agents de l'inspection du travail que le contrôle de l'application de la législation du travail devait s'exercer dans les professions artisanales. Ces instructions ont été reprises par une circulaire en date du 21 décembre 1974 confirmant qu'aucune disposition légale en vigueur ne permet d'exclure les salariés travaillant dans les entreprises artisanales du bénéfice des avantages

.../...

- 3 -

relatifs notamment aux conditions de travail et de rémunération, ou des mesures de protection et de prévention en matière d'hygiène et de sécurité.

Il existe donc au Maroc un ensemble complet de dispositions légales et administratives propres à instaurer dans les fabriques de tapis des conditions de travail conformes à la réglementation, particulièrement en ce qui concerne l'interdiction d'employer des enfants de moins de douze ans.

Il faut conclure que dans certains des établissements parmi ceux visités par les représentants de l'Association, cette réglementation n'est pas strictement appliquée, ce qui nécessite un contrôle plus efficace et plus soutenu.

3) En conséquence je donne toutes instructions utiles au Service de l'Inspection du travail afin d'une part, de faire procéder dans les meuilleurs délais à une enquête dans les établissements signalés par le rapport et assujettis à la législation en vigueur, d'autre part, de mettre en demeure le cas échéant, les employeurs concernés d'avoir à prendre toutes mesures appropriées pour assurer l'application de la législation dans leur entreprise.

4) Il importe cependant de préciser que la non application par quelques employeurs de certaines dispositions de la législation ne devrait pas conduire hâtivement à des appréciations générales dont la diffusion pourrait nuire à notre pays qui a mis en oeuvre des moyens non négligeables pour parvenir à la normalisation de situations particulières. La récente harmonisation légale des salaires du personnel féminin avec les salaires payés aux hommes dans des secteurs tels que notamment les industries textiles, offre un exemple caractéristique et positif de cette action.

.../...

- 4 -

        Il est à noter enfin, que le Ministère du travail et des affaires sociales n'a pas été appelé à participer à l'organisation de la visite au Maroc des représentants de l'Association, et n'a pu de ce fait leur fournir les informations nécessaires sur les modalités d'emploi et de travail dans le secteur d'activité concerné. De toute évidence ces informations auraient été de nature à donner un caractère plus objectif à certaines constations figurant dans le rapport établi par l'Association, qui ainsi, aurait reflété plus fidèlement la réalité de notre pays dans le domaine considéré.

        C'est pourquoi j'estime qu'une démarche pressante devrait être effectuée auprès de l'Organisation Internationale du travail et du Conseil Economique et Social des Nations Unies, afin d'informer ces organismes que le Gouvernement Marocain qui a pris connaissance avec toute l'attention requise du rapport de l'Association contre l'esclavage et pour la protection des droits de l'homme, ne juge pas opportun d'autoriser la publication éventuelle de ce rapport.

        J'adresse en conséquence copie de cette lettre à Messieurs les Représentants Permanents du Maroc à Genève et New-York en vue d'effectuer les démarches appropriées auprès des organisations internationales sus-nommées.

...../.....

5

II. SITUATION DES OUVRIERS TRAVAILLANT DANS LE SECTEUR ARTISANAL.

1) Période d'avant l'indépendance.

Au cours des années antérieures à l'indépendance, les entreprises artisanales n'étaient soumises, sur le plan social, à aucune des dispositions légales actuellement en vigueur.

Par circulaire en date du 11 Janvier 1952, il fut demandé aux agents de l'inspection du travail.
1°)- de contrôler les employeurs marocains installés en dehors des médinas.

2°)- de commencer par les industries et les commerces le plus évolués.

Mais la liste des employeurs Marocains non soumis au contrôle de l'inspection du travail, liste annexée à la circulaire précitée, englobait pratiquement toutes les industries et tous les commerces de caractère traditionnel ou artisanal installée en médinas, ou hors des médinas.

2) La Période d'après l'indépendance.

Après l'indépendance, il s'est posé la question de savoir s'il convenait d'appliquer la législation du travail aux établissements traditionnels ou artisanaux.

Il fut répondu à cette question par l'affirmative. En effet, en l'état actuel des textes, la législation du travail n'exclut pas de son champ d'application les entreprises artisanales sauf en ce qui concerne le régime de la sécurité sociale dont les conditions d'application aux salariés travaillant dans le secteur artisanal doivent être déterminées par decrét.

Néanmoins compte tenu de la situation particülière de ces entreprises, il a été demandé, par circulaire n° 56-32 du 11 Octobre 1956 aux agents de l'inspection du travail de faire en sorte que leur contrôle soit souple,

...../...

dans le but de parvenir à une application progressive de la législation du travail sans augmenter brusquement les charges des établissements artisanaux ou traditionnels.

2) <u>Evolution actuelle du Problème.</u>

Constatant que les entreprises artisanales semi-industrielles peuvent être largement soumises à l'ensemble des dispositions de la législation du travail, le Ministre du travail et des affaires sociales a invité de nouveau par circulaire n°4/74 du 21 décembre 1974 les agents de l'inspection du travail à contrôler efficacement ces entreprises.

Par ailleurs si pour des raisons économiques l'application intégrale de la législation au travail aux petits établissements artisanaux n'est pas souhaitable pour le moment il demeure néanmoins indispensable de déterminer un minimum de dispositions légales à faire observer par ces établissements car il est impensable de priver les ouvriers du secteur artisanal de la protection qu'assure la législation du travail aux salariés.

Il a donc été suggéré au Secrétariat d'Etat auprès du Premier Ministre Chargé de l'Entraide Nationale et de l'Artisanat qu'une réunion groupant les représentants de son département et ceux au Ministère du travail et des affaires sociales, se tienne le plutôt possible pour arrêter ce minimum et veiller à ce que les règles concernant l'hygiène et la moralité soient incluses.

Telle est l'évolution du problème se rapportant à l'application de la législation du travail dans le secteur artisanal qui, eu égard au nombre des ouvriers artisans, revêt une grande importance.

Le Gouvernement de Sa Majesté le Roi ne cesse de s'employer à aplanir la plupart des difficultés qui s'opposent actuellement à l'application de la législation du travail en vigueur, aux ouvriers relevant du secteur artisanal.

From: The Chairman of the Anti-Slavery Society
To: The First Secretary, Royal Moroccan Embassy, London

1 March 1976

Thank you for your letter of 14 January 1976, concerning working conditions in the carpet industry in Morocco. We welcome the positive reaction of the Ministry of Labour to our report, in particular the assurance that an enquiry will be made into the conditions described in our report, and that an inter-ministerial meeting will be held to discuss how to provide some legal protection for child workers in small artisan establishments. We congratulate the Moroccan government on this important step forward.

We would respectfully urge in this respect that the competent Ministry take into consideration during its deliberations the suggestions on page three of our report, that is to say the establishment of a list of all licensed employers of children who would be compelled to provide at least minimum standards of hygiene, light and space, the establishment of maximum hours of work for each age group, and the provision of some hours of education for children during working time in the factory.

If the Moroccan Government were to set up part-time schooling in the factories, we believe voluntary agencies in this country might contribute financial aid to such a programme; we would willingly support a request by the Moroccan Government to the voluntary agencies along these lines.

In view of the enlightened attitude of the Moroccan Government in this respect, we will gladly print the details given by the Ministry of Labour in your letter, and the assurances it contains, as a part of our final report on this matter.

Yours sincerely,

JEREMY SWIFT
Chairman

Mr Abdellatif Nacif
First Secretary
Royal Moroccan Embassy
49 Queen's Gate Gardens
London S W 7

ROYAL MOROCCAN EMBASSY

London, 14th June 1976.

49, QUEEN'S GATE GARDENS,
LONDON, S.W.7

01-584 8827/8

ECO/ca/ **000653**

Monsieur le Secrétaire Général de

L'Association Contre l'Esclavage
et pour la Protection des droits
de l'Homme,

60, Weymouth Street,
LONDON, W1N 4DX.

Objet : Conditions de travail dans les manufactures
de tapis au Maroc.

Référence : Votre correspondance N° UN/29 du 30 octobre
1975.
Ma lettre ECO/ca/ du 15 octobre 1975.
Ma lettre ECO/ca/00077 du 14 janvier 1976.

Suite à nos correspondances citées en référence,
cette Ambassade a l'honneur de vous faire parvenir, ci-joint,
un supplément d'information venant compléter les éléments
d'appréciations formulés par le Ministère Marocain du
travail et des Affaires Sociales, et relatifs aux condi-
-tions de travail dans les manufactures de tapis.

M. Abdellatif NACIF,
First Secretary.

- 2 -

Par ailleurs, des instructions ont d'ores et déjà été données à qui de droit aux fins de veiller au respect de la reglementation en vigueur et d'en assurer sa stricte observance.

A ces mesures d'ordre général, il ya lieu, d'ajouter les textes formant code de l'Artisanat à l'élaboration desquels mes services travaillent et qui, prévoyant l'immatriculation obligatoire de toutes les entreprises à caractère artisanal, permettront d'en recenser plus précisement le nombre et d'en contrôler beaucoup plus rigoureusement les conditions de fonctionnement.

Persuadé que l'ensemble des solutions envisagées va dans le sens de vos suggestions et, restant pleinement disposé à prendre en considération toute remarque suceptible de contribuer à rehausser davantage le prestige d'un secteur à l'épanouissement duquel mon département ne cesse d'oeuvrer, je vous prie de croire, Monsieur le Président, à l'assurance de ma haute considération.

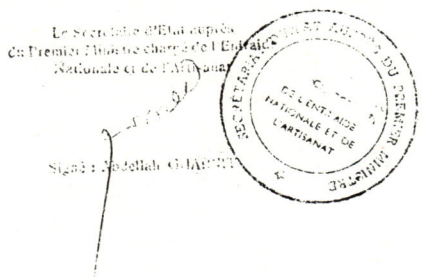

Le Secrétaire d'Etat auprès du Premier Ministre chargé de l'Entr'aide Nationale et de l'Artisanat

Signé : Abdellah CHARIF

...UME DU MAROC

PREMIER MINISTRE

SECRETARIAT D'ETAT
A L'ENTRAIDE NATIONALE
ET A L'ARTISANAT

6 joumada 1 1396

1 6 M 1975

المملكة المغربية

الوزير الاول

كتابة الدولة في التعاون الوطني
والصناعة التقليدية

LE SECRETAIRE D'ETAT AUPRES DU PREMIER MINISTRE
CHARGE DE L'ENTRAIDE NATIONALE ET DE L'ARTISANAT

J-2

/)/)ONSIEUR LE PRESIDENT DE LA **THE ANTI-SLAVERY**
SOCIETY 60 WEYMOUTH

LONDON, WIN 4 DX

S/C DE MONSIEUR LE MINISTRE D'ETAT CHARGE DES
AFFAIRES ETRANGERES

- RABAT -

_/)/)onsieur,

Vous avez bien voulu communiquer au grouvernement du Royaume du Maroc
sous forme de note, les constatations et observations qu'un groupe de votre
honorable association en mission dans mon pays pendant le mois de mars 1975
à recueillies relativement à la présence d'enfants-apprentis en formation dans
certaines entreprises artisanales placées sous l'autorité morale de ce Secrétariat
d'Etat chargé de l'Entraide Nationale et de l'Artisanat.

En vous remerciant bien vivement de cette initiative, je vous prie de
trouver ici l'expression des compliments de mon département pour les reflexions
pertinentes, objet de votre note d'où je n'ai pas manqué de relever avec satisfac-
tion, des commentaires favorables sur bon nombre d'établissements et de manufactures artisanaux.

Grand cas a été cependant fait des remarques formulées quant à l'emploi
quelque peu abusif des enfants d'âge scolaire dans des unités artisanales du
secteur privé et des conditions peu viables qui y prévalent en violation flagrante
des dispositions de notre législation considérée à juste titre comme une des
plus à l'avant-garde en matière de protection sociale.

A cet égard, il conviendrait de vous signaler que des réunions groupant les
départements intéressés se tiennent en vue de mettre un terme aux cas signalés et
dégager des solutions de nature à conserver intact le prestige de ce secteur et
à sauvegarder l'image de marque de ses produits à l'étranger.

../..

27th October 1977.

His Excellency
The Ambassador of Morocco,
49 Queen's Gate Gardens,
London, S.W.7.

Your Excellency,

      I have the honour to refer to my letter of 17th June 1977 with which were enclosed two copies of a report prepared in 1977 by this Society on the conditions in carpet factories employing children in your Country.

      I said that it was my Committee's intention to publish the report in due course and added that if your Government so wished, we would publish its comments together with the report.

      My Committee is now ready to publish the report and would thus be grateful to know – may I say by 8th November ? – whether or not it is your Government's intention to accept the Society's offer to include its comments when publishing the report. If your Government does intend to accept this offer we shall be grateful if those comments could reach this office by 8th December 1977.

      I have the honour to be

         Your Excellency's humble servant,

         SECRETARY